revive my heart!

revive my heart!

SATISFY YOUR THIRST FOR PERSONAL SPIRITUAL REVIVAL

"If anyone is thirsty, let him come to me and drink.
Whoever believes in me, as the Scripture has said,
streams of living water will flow from within him."
JOHN 7:37-38 (NIV)

catherine martin

NAVPRESS

Bringing Truth to Life
P.O. Box 35001, Colorado Springs, Colorado 80935

OUR GUARANTEE TO YOU

We believe so strongly in the message of our books that we are making this quality guarantee to you. If for any reason you are disappointed with the content of this book, return the title page to us with your name and address and we will refund to you the list price of the book. To help us serve you better, please briefly describe why you were disappointed. Mail your refund request to: NavPress, P.O. Box 35002, Colorado Springs, CO 80935.

The Navigators is an international Christian organization. Our mission is to reach, disciple, and equip people to know Christ and to make Him known through successive generations. We envision multitudes of diverse people in the United States and every other nation who have a passionate love for Christ, live a lifestyle of sharing Christ's love, and multiply spiritual laborers among those without Christ.

NavPress is the publishing ministry of The Navigators. NavPress publications help believers learn biblical truth and apply what they learn to their lives and ministries. Our mission is to stimulate spiritual formation among our readers.

Cover design by David Carlson Design
Cover photo by Susan Findlay/Masterfile
Creative Team: Terry Behimer, Karen Lee-Thorp, Amy Spencer, Pat Miller

Some of the anecdotal illustrations in this book are true to life and are included with the permission of the persons involved. All other illustrations are composites of real situations, and any resemblance to people living or dead is coincidental.

Unless otherwise identified, all Scripture quotations in this publication are taken from the *New American Standard Bible* (NASB), © The Lockman Foundation 1960, 1962, 1963, 1968, 1971, 1972, 1973, 1975, 1977, 1995. Other versions used are the HOLY BIBLE: NEW INTERNATIONAL VERSION® (NIV®), Copyright © 1973, 1978, 1984 by International Bible Society, used by permission of Zondervan Publishing House, all rights reserved; *The Message: New Testament with Psalms and Proverbs* (MSG) by Eugene H. Peterson, copyright © 1993, 1994, 1995, used by permission of NavPress Publishing Group; *The Living Bible* (TLB), copyright © 1971, used by permission of Tyndale House Publishers, Inc., Wheaton, IL 60189, all rights reserved; the *Amplified New Testament* (AMP), © The Lockman Foundation 1954, 1958; the *Williams New Testament* (WMS) by Charles B. Williams, © 1937, 1965, 1966, by Edith S. Williams, Moody Bible Institute of Chicago; the *Holy Bible, New Living Translation* (NLT), copyright © 1996. Used by permission of Tyndale House Publishers, Inc., Wheaton, Illinois 60189. All rights reserved; and the *King James Version* (KJV).

Every effort has been made to locate the owners of copyrighted materials in this publication. Upon notification, the publisher will make proper correction in subsequent printings.

Excerpts from the following have been reprinted with the generous permission of the publisher: *THEY FOUND THE SECRET* by Mrs. Victor Raymond Edman. Copyright © 1960 by Zondervan Publishing House. Used by permission of Zondervan Publishing House. *Page 88*; THE INNER LIFE, by Andrew Murray. Copyright © 1980 by Zondervan Corporation. Used by permission of Zondervan Publishing House. Pages 68-69; MATTHEW HENRY'S COMMENTARY OF THE WHOLE BIBLE by Leslie F. Church; Gerald W. Peterman. Copyright © 1991 by Harper Collins Publishers Ltd. Used by permission of Zondervan Publishing House. Page 1555; THE SAVING LIFE OF CHRIST, by W. Ian Thomas. Copyright © 1961 by Zondervan Publishing House. Used by permission of Zondervan Publishing House. Page 19; THE BLESSINGS OF BROKENNESS, by Charles F. Stanley. Copyright © 1997 by Charles F. Stanley. Used by permission of Zondervan Publishing House. Pages 102-103. All other permissions are cited in Notes.

Printed in the United States of America

3 4 5 6 7 8 9 10 / 11 10 09 08 07

FOR A FREE CATALOG OF
NAVPRESS BOOKS & BIBLE STUDIES,
CALL 1-800-366-7788 (USA)
OR 1-800-839-4769 (CANADA)

Dedicated to . . .
the Reviver of my heart,
my Lord Jesus Christ,
who has faithfully given me
everything I've needed
for every situation of life.

The staff of Campus Crusade for Christ

Dr. Bill Bright, founder and president,
Campus Crusade for Christ,
who has taught me by example
to believe God for the impossible
and to live in the power of the Holy Spirit.

Josh and Dottie McDowell,
who have stood as examples to me
of true servants of our Lord.

Bob Tiede, director of Josh McDowell Ministry,
and my director while on staff
with Campus Crusade for Christ,
who taught me faithfulness in ministry.

Elmer Lappen, former CCC Director at ASU,
who taught me that knowing God in His Word
was the most important thing I could give myself to in life.

Leann Pruitt McGee, former CCC staff member,
who taught me early on about personal spiritual revival
through quiet time with our Lord.

contents

foreword

Nothing is more important in our Christian walk than our intimacy with the Lord. This involves worshiping and praising Him, listening to His voice, reading and meditating on His Word, sharing our hearts with Him, and interceding for needs He shares with us.

Such intimacy is much more important than outward activities that we may perform in "Christian service," needful as they may be. Even though good and well meaning, unless our activities spring forth out of communion with Him, they are likely not to be Spirit-led and may be fruitless. Jesus said, "I am the vine; you are the branches. Those who remain in me, and I in them, will produce much fruit. For apart from me you can do nothing" (John 15:5, NLT).

Let me give you a powerful example. Prayer and devotions have always been top priority in the lives of my beloved wife, Vonette, and me. A most memorable occasion was in the spring of 1951, when Vonette and I got on our knees in our home and prayed. This was a very special and unique devotional time that changed our lives and that, by His grace, the Lord has used to touch literally billions of people all over the world with His message of love and forgiveness. We prayed, "Lord, we surrender our lives irrevocably to you and to do your will. We want to love and serve you with all of our hearts for the rest of our lives." We actually wrote and signed a contract committing our whole lives to Him, relinquishing all of our rights, all of our possessions, everything we would ever own, giving Him, our dear Lord and Master, everything. That Sunday afternoon, in the words of the apostle Paul, Vonette and I became voluntary slaves of Jesus, by choice, as an act of our wills. In Romans 1:1, Paul wrote of his love for Christ and said to the Christians in that great city: "This letter is from Paul, Jesus Christ's slave, chosen to be a missionary, and sent out to preach God's Good News" (TLB).

Astonishingly, within twenty-four hours of that prayer and in another quiet time, the Lord gave me the vision for Campus Crusade for Christ and helping to fulfill the Great Commission! Every quiet time may not produce a result that dramatic, but let us not limit what God can do in our own lives. He is always full of surprises! The most important thing is that we get to know Him. "Now this is eternal life: that they may know you, the only true God, and Jesus Christ, whom you have sent" (John 17:3, NIV).

This outstanding devotional book will help you know Him better. It has been a great honor to have served the Lord with Catherine Martin when she was associated with Campus Crusade for Christ, and I am deeply moved by the remarkable things He has done in her life since then and the wonderful insights God has given her on this important subject.

DR. BILL BRIGHT
Founder and President
Campus Crusade for Christ International

acknowledgments

Thank you, first of all, to my beloved husband, David Martin, M.D., who has been more supportive of me than any woman could hope for in life. Thank you, David, for all the dinners you cooked, for all the editing you have done, for listening to me go on and on about ideas, and for pulling me away from the computer to play golf when I needed a rest. I love you with all my heart.

Thank you to my mother, Elizabeth Snyder, for loving me and always being so excited when I call to say, "Guess what just happened!" Thank you for sharing my heart of hearts. Thank you to my dad, Bob Snyder, for teaching me to go for it in life and never give up. To Rob, the best brother any girl could have, thank you for being such a discerning listener and for teaching me about surrender to the Lord. Tania, you and Christopher bring such joy to my heart. Kayla, my precious niece, you are the apple of my eye and have added a whole new dimension to my life. I love you. Eloise, thank you for loving the Lord and encouraging me. Andy, Ann, Keegan, James—thank you for your love. Nana, I love you.

Thank you to Andy Kotner for being with me through thick and thin. What a gift from the Lord you are. Thank you for always being there and for laughing and crying with me. Thank you, Beverly Trupp, for encouraging and inspiring me to dare to dream big with the Lord. I love our long talks. Thank you to Shirley Guy and Bill Ervin for being such good friends and for brainstorming ideas with me.

Conni Hudson, thank you for being my heart friend, for encouraging me in the hard times and cheering me on to write these books of quiet times. You know I never could have done it without you. You are one of God's great gifts to me. Thank you for leading the pilot study of *Revive My Heart!* It was a grand adventure. Thank you to all the women who piloted *Revive My Heart!*: Conni Hudson, Janet Teuerle, Melissa Brown, Debra Collins, Debbie Griffin, Beverly Trupp, Kelly Abeyratne, Connie Sparks, Cindy Clark, Sharon Hastings, Myra Murphy, Cheryl Beaver, Julie Brauckmann, Vicki Kelly, Gayle Bourgeois, Sue Meyers, Heather Miller, Bobbie Teague, Paula U'Ren, Mary Diamon, Davida Kreisler, Dawn Ivie, Carla Colburn, and Belva Dickinson. Cindy Clark, thank you for being such a true friend. You have assisted me in every aspect of ministry this year. I so appreciate your faithfulness to the Lord and your encouragement in my life.

A special thank you to Kelly Abeyratne, who has been my prayer warrior in ministry and has encouraged me to keep running this race that is set before us. Thank you to Myra Murphy and Carla Colburn for dreaming with me about the Revive My Heart Conferences. Thank you to Kayla, my assistant, for being a steadfast servant of the Lord. Thank you, Karen Mounce, for typing and organizing the numerous permissions to quote. You are an incredible servant of the Lord. Thank you to Belva Dickinson for assisting me in numerous projects in our office. A special thank you to Linda Nichols for encouraging me in the writing of this book. And thank you, Wendy Jones, for loaning me *Keswick's Authentic Voice* for the entire summer. I can give it back to you now because I finally found one for my library!

And then, thank you to the pastors and the staff at Southwest Community Church, who are such a joy to serve the Lord with in ministry. Thank you, Stefanie Kelly, for writing incredible music and ministering to so many, including me, when you sing. Thank you to the women at Southwest Community Church, who are my great joy! You have the greatest hearts for the Lord and challenge me onward in this adventure of knowing God.

Thank you to NavPress for being a publisher committed to the Lord Jesus Christ. Special thanks to Kent Wilson, Terry Behimer, Dan Rich, and Toben Heim. Also, thank you to Karen Lee-Thorp for your help in editing. Thank you to Amy Spencer for your great attention to detail and your gracious help in the publishing of this book. A special thanks to Jack Smith, publisher at Banner Of Truth Trust, for that day on the phone when you encouraged me in the publishing of these books.

Thank you to those who partner with me in Quiet Time Ministries to help with the daily operations of this work that God is using worldwide to teach devotion to God and His Word. None of this could happen without you! Thank you to the board of directors for being such great advisors in the movement and direction of Quiet Time Ministries: Conni Hudson, Shirley Peters, Jane Lyons, and my husband. Thank you to my magazine staff with Quiet Time Ministries: Shirley Peters, Cay Hough, Maurine Cromwell, Laurie Bailey, and Conni Hudson, who have explored many of these thoughts on personal spiritual revival with me in our magazines.

what is on the heart of God today?

It was my last year of college. I had the wonderful opportunity to attend a Christmas conference sponsored by Campus Crusade for Christ at Arrowhead Springs, nestled in the mountains of southern California. The main speaker for this conference was Elmer Lappen, director of Campus Crusade for Christ at Arizona State University. I was sitting in a room with a thousand other students from all over the United States, listening to Elmer give his characteristic final challenge on the last day of his series on discipleship. At the end of his message, he outlined the call that God gave to Isaiah in Isaiah 6:8: "Then I heard the voice of the LORD, saying, 'Whom shall I send, and who will go for Us?'" Isaiah responded, "Here am I. Send me!" Those words altered the course of his life.

As Elmer explained Isaiah's heart response, he said that he was going to issue the same call to us. I listened with anticipation. My heart raced. This was what God had been building up to in my own life for two years. I had surrendered my life to the Lord at the end of my third year in college. The following year I had gotten involved in Campus Crusade for Christ and had been taught by Leann, one of their staff members. She showed me how to have a quiet time, and I learned to draw near to God daily in prayer and study of His Word. As I spent daily time with God, I grew to love His Word. I would spend hours underlining verses and thinking about their meaning and relevance in my own life.

It was such an exciting time. All I wanted was to live for Jesus Christ with a passionate and wholehearted devotion to Him. And now, here I was at the last Christmas conference before college graduation. Elmer Lappen said that if we wanted to be sold out to Jesus Christ, to go where He led and do what He asked, that we were to stand, state our name, and say, "Here am I, Lord. Send me." It was a moment etched in time for me. Elmer issued his call. I watched as young people all around the room began to stand, state their names, and respond to God. My heart was beating fast. Now was the time for me. I stood and said, "My name is Catherine. Here am I, Lord. Send me!" By the time it was over, there were a thousand young men and women standing tall for Jesus Christ. That group included me. I'll never forget it.

That was twenty-two years ago. That response to God altered the course of my life. It became the determining factor in everything I have done over the years. God has been in the business of making me a surrendered, sold-out servant and radical disciple of Jesus Christ. He is still doing His work in me. There have been times when I have been tempted to give up because the fiery trial has been so hot. There have been times when I have given in to despair and discouragement. And there have been high times of triumph and victory when I have seen God do what only He can do. I have discovered that following Jesus Christ is not just another way to live. It is the *only* way to live. And it is, as Corrie ten Boom used to say, a fantastic adventure in trusting Him.

Jesus said that in the last days "many will turn away from the faith" and "the love of most will grow cold" (Matthew 24:10,12, NIV). I believe we are living in a time when what Jesus described is now happening in our world. I believe that we are living in a world that is in trouble. When is a world in trouble? When it is no longer outraged over immorality. When it is more afraid of governments than of God. When the computer consumes more time than Christ. When the most popular book on knowing God contains very little mention of Jesus Christ. When prayer becomes optional in the church. When worship of God is considered intolerant and narrow. When the church is no longer different from the world. When pursuit of the good life takes precedence over pursuit of God. When its greatest heroes are people whose personal lives are in disarray. That is when a world is in trouble.

In *The God of All Comfort,* Hannah Whitall Smith described a conversation she had with an intelligent agnostic she very much wanted to influence. He listened to her for a while and then said,

> Well madam, all I have to say is this. If you Christians want to make us agnostics inclined to look into your religion, you must try to be more comfortable in the possession of it yourselves. The Christians I meet seem to me to be the very most uncomfortable people anywhere around. They seem to carry their religion as a man carries a headache. He does not want to get rid of his head, but at the same time it is very uncomfortable to have it. And I for one do not care to have that sort of religion.

Why are Christians so uncomfortable these days? I believe that it is because they are desperately in need of personal revival. So many have barren hearts that can be traced back to a neglect of God and His Word. The busyness of life has simply crowded God out of most lives. One thing you can count on: If you are superficial with God and His Word, you will be a superficial Christian who is easily swayed and compromised. If you will plumb the depths of God through consistent study of His Word and through prayer, then you will have spiritual depth that draws upon your heavenly Father's resources in times of trouble (see Jeremiah 17:5-8).

I see so many believers falling by the wayside these days. The fiery trials have come upon them, and in their own strength they have been unable to bear the pain. Life can be unbearable and uncertain at times. How can anyone experience the victorious, abundant life that Jesus promised? It is possible in only one way: personal spiritual revival.

I believe God is issuing a call to you and me for such a time as this. What will your answer be? God is calling you to one thing: personal spiritual revival. What does it mean to be revived? Personal revival is a quickening of heart and soul by God, imparting whatever is necessary to sustain one's spiritual life and enable a return to the experience of one's true purpose as ordained by God. God's purpose for you is that you might know Him and make Him known. He desires an intimate relationship with you. Then, He desires that you live for Him in this world. As you live in His power and strength, you will make an incredible difference in the world. Personal spiritual revival brings you to the place where you say along with Isaiah: "Here am I. Send me!" It has been said that the world has yet to see what God can do in and through the lives of those whose hearts are wholly yielded to Him. This is what I believe is on the heart of God. He repeats this message throughout His Word. I believe personal revival has always been on God's heart.

This book of quiet times has a single aim and focus: that you might grow up into Jesus Christ and become His radical disciple, willing to sacrifice all to follow Him. What is the secret to such a life? To draw near to Him, day by day, listening to what He says in His Word, talking to Him, and being consistently and powerfully transformed into the person He wants you to be. That is the secret of personal spiritual revival.

Together we will embark on this journey through Scripture in the form of quiet times alone with the Lord. The quiet times are organized according to the plan that was developed and is taught by Quiet Time Ministries: P.R.A.Y.E.R.™ Each day this plan will include:

Prepare your heart
Read and study God's Word
Adore God in prayer
Yield yourself to God
Enjoy His presence
Rest in His love[1]

Each quiet time includes devotional reading, devotional Bible study, journaling, prayer, worship, meditating on hymns, and application of God's Word in your life. In the back of this book, you will find Journal Pages and Prayer Pages for you to record your thoughts and prayers. With this book and your Bible you have everything you need for your quiet time with the Lord.

This book is designed to be flexible. Because schedules vary, you may choose to take more than one day for each quiet time. You may do each quiet time at your own pace, taking as little or as much time as you can give to spend alone with the Lord.

You may choose to lead a group using *Revive My Heart!* There is a leader's guide with discussion questions and accompanying messages on audiotape and videotape available from Quiet Time Ministries or online at www.quiettime.org.

Wherever you are, stop now and ask the Lord to begin His reviving, spiritual work in you. Pray that wonderful prayer: *Revive my heart.* Then get ready. Something extraordinary is just around the corner.

the promise of revival

week
one

JOHN 7:37-39

are you thirsty?

"If anyone is thirsty . . . "
JOHN 7:37

Prepare Your Heart

Two thousand years ago, a light dawned upon earth that altered the course of human life. God in Christ came to dwell with His people, to display His glory, to die so that He might give His beloved ones forgiveness of sins and eternal life, to rise from the dead, and to ascend to heaven that He might be with them forever. When He entered human history in time and space, He found a people who were lost, hurting, aimless. These people flocked to hear Him because His words offered more than just hope. They were filled with life. The Lord Jesus knew the human dilemma, for He knew the hearts of men and women. He created them. And He created them to be filled with only one thing: Himself. Only God is big enough to fill a human heart. Apart from God, there is a need that is often described in the Bible as thirst. It is a thirst for total forgiveness, unconditional love, and eternal life. Ultimately, it is a thirst for God. Only God can answer the thirst of men and women.

As you begin this study on personal spiritual revival, draw near to God and be still in His presence. The question to think about is the question God asked Adam and Eve: "Where are you?" How is your relationship with the Lord? Have you been spending time with Him consistently? How is your quiet time? What has God been teaching you in the last six months?

Turn to Psalm 40 and meditate on the words as a preparation of heart. Then take the next few moments to write a prayer to the Lord in the form of a letter, asking Him to speak to you during your study in *Revive My Heart!* in such a way as to change your life. Ask Him to do a mighty work in you as you spend time with Him in His Word. You may use the space provided on the next page to write your letter to God.

LETTER TO GOD

"Call to me and I will answer you and tell you great and unsearchable things you do not know" (Jeremiah 33:3, NIV).

READ AND STUDY GOD'S WORD

This week, as a preparation for your study on personal spiritual revival, you are going to look at the promise of revival that is found throughout God's Word. You will discover that God's plan for you is an extraordinary, abundant life. So many people do not experience what God has in mind for them. So many walk in a dry and weary land where there is no water. The refrain is often, "Is that all there is?" There is a deep thirst within, but no personal satisfaction. There is very little experience of God as described in His Word. God knows this, so He makes it clear that much more is available.

1. The main passage of Scripture that you will meditate on this week is John 7:37-39. Read these words of Jesus and imagine that you are in the crowd. You are surrounded by people who have many different feelings about Jesus' identity. Some believe He is the promised Messiah who will save His people from their sins. Others believe He is a conquering king who will rule the world. Others think He is a prophet. Others are threatened by His presence and want to destroy Him. Others are unsure as to who He is but want to hear what He has to say. As you read His words, think about who you say Jesus is.

2. Write out Jesus' words in 7:37-39.

3. What do you think Jesus is promising in these statements?

4. Who can experience the fulfillment of His promise?

5. This invitation to those who are thirsty comes from God and is found throughout His Word. Look at the following verses and record what you learn about the human condition and about God's invitation and promises to you.
   Isaiah 41:17-20

Matthew 5:6

John 4:4-15

John 6:35

Revelation 7:14-17

Revelation 21:6

Optional verses: If you have additional time to spend in God's Word, you may look at Isaiah 42:10-16; 43:15-25; 44:3; 49:8-16; 55:1. You may use your Journal Pages in the back of this book to record each passage and your insights. If you cannot look at these optional verses today, you may choose to return to them on days 6–7 of this week.

6. From the verses you studied, summarize in two or three sentences your most significant insights related to the thirst of people and the promise of God.

ADORE GOD IN PRAYER

In what ways are you thirsty today? Ask the Lord to answer the thirst of your heart with Himself. You may choose to use the Prayer Pages in the back of this study book to record your prayer.

YIELD YOURSELF TO GOD

There are some who believe that Christ has offered in His gospel more than He has to give. People admit that they have not experienced what was predicted as the portion of the children of God. But why is this so? Has the Kingdom of God been over-advertised or is it only that it has been under-believed? Has the Lord Jesus Christ been over-estimated, or has He only been under-trusted? I firmly believe that the Kingdom of God could not possibly be over-advertised nor the Lord Jesus Christ over-estimated. *Eye hath not seen, nor ear heard, neither have entered into the heart of man, the things which God hath prepared for them that love Him* (I Cor. 2:9 NASB). All the difficulty arises from the fact that we have under-believed and under-trusted. In the Lord Jesus Christ, there is a deep and lasting peace and comfort of soul which nothing earthly can disturb. It belongs to those who embrace it. If this is our rightful portion, we must learn how to receive it and what things hinder its becoming a reality in our lives.

HANNAH WHITALL SMITH IN *THE GOD OF ALL COMFORT*

The blessing that I need is actually here for me, and God intends me to have it. He does not mock the desire of the heart that He has made by empty rhetoric, by sounding phrases, by beautiful poetry, by the imagery that charms our fancy. Ah, no! God does not deal in mere tropes when He offers to us the realities of the Kingdom of heaven—*if any man thirst, let him come unto me, and drink.* . . . If any of us are thirsting, Jesus is here. He is just calling to the thirsty one, and He is saying, "you are not only going to drink—you are going to do that—but I am going to so fill you with myself and with my Holy Spirit, that forth from you the living water shall flow." . . . You who have said "I have no sort of influence," are going to find a new and wonderful influence, working through your weakness, for the glory of God and the salvation of man. Do you believe it.[1]

CANON W. HAY H. M. AITKEN, M.A., IN *KESWICK'S AUTHENTIC VOICE*

Take heart today if you are thirsty for the Lord. Blessed are you; according to the Lord's promise in Matthew 5:6, you will be satisfied.

ENJOY HIS PRESENCE
What has touched you the most in today's study? Write out one thought, insight, or verse in your Journal in the back of this book, and carry that truth with you throughout the day.

REST IN HIS LOVE
"Ho! Every one who thirsts, come to the waters" (Isaiah 55:1).

come to Jesus

" . . . let him come to Me."
JOHN 7:37

Prepare Your Heart

Where do you run in life—for rest, for refreshment, for satisfaction, for help in a time of trouble? In the midst of all your responsibilities, circumstances, conflicts, and cares, there is a standing invitation to you from Jesus Christ, the King of kings and Lord of lords. He says, "Come to Me." Will you go to Him? The world demands that you work harder and faster so that you can add more to your already growing list of responsibilities. Jesus bids you to lay aside those things for a time, withdraw, find a quiet place, and draw near to Him. Never is your need for time with Him greater than if you are involved not only in job and family responsibilities, but also in a ministry.

Jesus sent His twelve disciples to go two by two to towns, preaching a message of repentance. It was an incredible challenge for them. The trip was successful—"they drove out many demons and anointed many sick people with oil and healed them" (Mark 6:13, NIV). It was exciting to return and tell Jesus what had happened. However, as often happens on ministry trips, they were so busy they hardly had time to eat. Jesus' response to their weariness has implications for your own life. He said to His disciples, "Come with me by yourselves to a quiet place and get some rest" (Mark 6:31, NIV).

Understand this: Jesus' priority is always quiet time with Him. Neglect of drawing near to Him will certainly result in arriving at a dry and weary land, desperately in need of personal spiritual revival. It is critical to learn to find quiet time with the Lord. It is imperative that you have a time, a place, and a plan for your quiet time.

First, the time. There is no appointment more important than the one you make with your Lord every day. He is your Master, the Creator of the universe, certainly more important than any earthly CEO. Yet how often is that appointment with the Lord missed? Personal

revival will begin and continue in your life when you resolve to spend time with God in His
Word every day. Choose a time each day when you can be alone with God. It should be a
time when you are alert and not distracted. A time when you can truly draw near to the Lord
in uninterrupted prayer and meditation in His Word.

Then, the place. Where do you spend time with God? Is it on the run, driving in your car,
five minutes before work? Sometimes those are the only moments in certain days to slip away
and be alone with the Lord. It is important to find a quiet place that becomes your place of
retreat—a place where you run to be alone with Him. You can keep all your quiet time materials in that place, on a shelf or table, or even in a basket.

Finally, the plan. What are you going to do in your quiet time with the Lord? That is the
purpose of *Revive My Heart!*—to give you a plan for your quiet time that includes devotional
reading and Bible study, hymns, journaling, prayer, worship, and much more. This plan will
help you develop new ideas for your quiet time and become consistent along the way.

As you draw near to the Lord today, resolve to make time alone with Him a priority so
you can experience the adventure of knowing God. Take a few moments and ask the Lord to
quiet your heart and speak to you as you pray and read His Word.

READ AND STUDY GOD'S WORD
Today you will think about what it really means to come to Jesus and drink.

1. Read John 7:37-38 again. Imagine that Jesus is saying those words directly to you.
Write down any new insights from this passage.

2. Over and over, Jesus invited others to *come to Him*. And people came to Him from
everywhere. When they did, their lives were changed. Look at the following verses and
record your insights about the Jesus' character, His invitation, and the results of coming
to Him.

Mark 6:30-32

Matthew 11:28-30 (see also Jeremiah 31:25)

John 1:9-14

John 6:44-51

John 8:12

John 10:7-11

John 14:6

John 15:5

Revelation 3:20

3. Summarize what you have learned today about Jesus Christ, what it means to come to Him, and what will happen as a result.

ADORE GOD IN PRAYER

Look back over the truths you have learned about Christ today. Take each truth about your Lord, personalize it, and use the words to form a prayer of thanksgiving and praise to Him. For example, "Lord, thank you that when I believe in You, I will never thirst again" or "Lord, thank you that You stand at the door of my heart. Lord, today I open that door. Come in and dine with me. What a joy it is that I may spend time with You today!"

YIELD YOURSELF TO GOD

What do you suppose was the attraction that caused the Galilean fishermen to leave their nets and follow Jesus? What made Levi the tax collector abandon his booth and cash box to join His team? One answer might be: Jesus was a man of such joy, such merriment, such gladness of Spirit, such freedom and openness that He was irresistible. Today that may seem hard to visualize, but in ancient Palestine it is clear that people wanted to be near Him, to catch His bright spirit, and if possible to learn His secret, to share His joy and join in what He was doing for other people.[1]

SHERWOOD E. WIRT IN *JESUS MAN OF JOY*

Christ's Love is like torrential waters. His Grace is like a swelling tide. Who can approach the height and depth, length and breadth of the Love of God? It passeth understanding; it is beyond our comprehension, but from it comes that life-giving stream from which you and I find refreshment. God's Word, too, is like a great torrent. The depths of its mysteries will never be fathomed, the height of its glory never attained, the vastness of its wonders never discovered. It is a mine never to be exhausted, a spring never to run dry. It is the unsearchable riches of His grace but, whilst it remains beyond all human comprehension, we thank God for the still waters of that Word to which we have been led and of which we have partaken, and we shall anticipate the day when we shall be able to eat of the hidden manna and drink of the fountain head.[2]

CHARLES W. SLEMMING IN *HE RESTORETH MY SOUL*

Will you draw near today to the most amazing Person in the world, the Lord Jesus Christ, and spend some time with Him? Give Him your every care and need. If you have never established a relationship with the Lord, you may do so now by praying a very simple prayer: *Lord Jesus, I need you. Thank you for dying on the cross for my sins. I invite you now to come into my life, forgive my sins, and give me eternal life. In Jesus' name. Amen.* You can know by the promise in John 1:12 that all who receive the Lord Jesus Christ are given the right to become children of God, and according to John 3:16, whoever believes in Him will never perish but will inherit eternal life.

ENJOY HIS PRESENCE

As you close your time with the Lord today, meditate on the words of this hymn and direct it as a prayer to your Lord.

Jesus, Lover of My Soul

Jesus, lover of my soul, let me to thy bosom fly,
while the nearer waters roll, while the tempest still is high.

Hide me, O my Savior, hide, till the storm of life is past;
safe into the haven guide; O receive my soul at last.

Other refuge have I none, hangs my helpless soul on thee;
leave, ah! leave me not alone, still support and comfort me.
All my trust on thee is stayed, all my help from thee I bring;
cover my defenseless head with the shadow of thy wing.

Thou, O Christ, art all I want, more than all in thee I find;
raise the fallen, cheer the faint, heal the sick, and lead the blind.
Just and holy is thy name, I am all unrighteousness;
false and full of sin I am; thou art full of truth and grace.

Plenteous grace with thee is found, grace to cover all my sin;
let the healing streams abound, make and keep me pure within.
Thou of life the fountain art, freely let me take of thee;
spring thou up within my heart; rise to all eternity.

CHARLES WESLEY

REST IN HIS LOVE

"Are you tired? Worn out? Burned out on religion? Come to me. Get away with me and you'll recover your life. I'll show you how to take a real rest. Walk with me and work with me — watch how I do it. Learn the unforced rhythms of grace. I won't lay anything heavy or ill-fitting on you. Keep company with me and you'll learn to live freely and lightly" (Matthew 11:28-29, MSG).

fill your cup with living water

". . . let him come to Me and drink."
JOHN 7:37

Prepare Your Heart

Worldliness and religious indifference dominated Wales in the late 1800s. Yet certain church leaders were burdened by this sad state of affairs. The burden led them to pray more fervently. They longed for a gracious outpouring of the Holy Spirit to descend upon them.

A minister named Joseph Jenkins pleaded for the anointing of the Holy Spirit on his own life. The result was such boldness and power that his ministry was transformed. He began to lead conferences in January 1904. A tremendous longing for the filling of the Holy Spirit began to spread through these meetings. Seth Joshua, an itinerant evangelist, arrived in the area and said, "I have never seen the power of the Holy Spirit so powerfully manifested among the people as at this place just now."

For the next year and a half, the Holy Spirit was poured out in Wales, and the hearts of men and women were awakened all across that land. The event has become known as the Welsh Revival of 1904–1905. During the Welsh Revival, there were times when services continued for four or five hours as people were moved to plead for mercy, and they stayed into the early hours of the morning, praying for the Holy Spirit to work in them.

The same God who caused the Welsh Revival can once again pour out His Spirit in an extraordinary way. God wants to fill you with His Holy Spirit today and every day in such a way that you will live the abundant life that He has promised you. Today, as you draw near to God, turn to Ephesians 3:20. Think about these words of Paul, and then ask the Lord to do more in your life than you can ask or imagine, according to the power that works within you.

READ AND STUDY GOD'S WORD

You have been looking at the incredible words of Jesus in John 7:37-38. These words take on new meaning when you understand their background. Jesus exclaimed this great promise on the last day of the Feast of Tabernacles. On each of the first seven days of the feast, a priest would draw water from the pool of Siloam, bring it to the temple, and pour it into a bowl beside the altar. This ceremony symbolized thanksgiving for God's mercies in giving water in the past and included prayer for future provision. Isaiah 12:3 is associated with this ceremony: "You will joyously draw water from the springs of salvation." The Jerusalem Talmud (the definitive Jewish commentary on the Law of Moses, put in writing in the first few centuries A.D.) connects the Feast of Tabernacles and Isaiah 12:3 with the Holy Spirit.[1] Jesus spoke His words of hope with this symbolism in mind.

Further, on the eighth day of the feast, the priest poured no water. That was the day on which Jesus stood and cried out these words. Turn to John 7:37-38 and read again what Jesus said, thinking about the background of His statements.

1. According to John 7:39, what do you drink when you come to Jesus?

2. Jesus is speaking of the powerful ministry of the Holy Spirit in the lives of believers. It is impossible to talk about personal spiritual revival without talking about the Holy Spirit. It is by the outpouring of God's Spirit that personal revival takes place. Take some time now to think about the Holy Spirit. Who is the third Person of the Trinity, the Holy Spirit? What is His ministry? If you are short on time, choose two or three of the following passages.

John 14:16-17

John 14:26

John 16:7-15

Acts 1:8

Romans 5:5

Romans 8:13-16

Romans 8:26-27

1 Corinthians 2:9-12

Galatians 5:22-25

Ephesians 3:16

Ephesians 5:18

3. What is the most significant insight you have learned about the Holy Spirit today?

ADORE GOD IN PRAYER

Ask the Lord Jesus to fill you with His Holy Spirit today. The word *drink* in John 7:37 is in the present imperative tense, which means it is a command and a continuous, repeated action. Day by day, the Lord wants to fill you with His Holy Spirit as you come to Him to drink of His Spirit. To be filled means to be controlled and empowered by the Lord Jesus Christ. Make this your one great prayer today—that the Lord would fill you with His Holy Spirit.

Yield Yourself to God

The God-honoring quality of life is always the divine objective in the believer's daily life. Its realization is never by a human resolution or struggle or the resources of the flesh; it is by *fighting the good fight of faith*. There is a wide difference between *fighting* to do what God alone can do, and *fighting* to maintain an attitude of dependence on Him to do what He alone can do. The child of God has an all-engaging responsibility of continuing in an attitude of reliance upon the Spirit. This is the point of his constant attention. This is his divinely appointed task and place of co-operation in the mighty undertakings of God. The locomotive engineer will accomplish little when pushing his ponderous train. He is not appointed to such a service. His real usefulness will begin when he takes his place at the throttle. The important conflict in the believer's life is to maintain the unbroken attitude of reliance upon the Spirit. Thus, and only thus, can the Spirit possess and vitalize every human faculty, emotion and choice.

LEWIS SPERRY CHAFER IN *HE THAT IS SPIRITUAL*

It is a remarkable conception—the life of God in me, so that I live as He lives; the wisdom of God in me, so that I see as He sees; the love of God in me, so that I desire what He desires; the victory of God in me, so that I win as He wins—that is the effect of the reception of the Holy Spirit.[2]

REV. A. T. PIERSON IN *KESWICK'S AUTHENTIC VOICE*

Enjoy His Presence
Are you aware of the presence of the Lord in your life today? And that He loves you and delights in you? Are you relying on His strength and provision for your needs? Are you noticing incredible things in His Word? Do you feel drawn to pray? If so, then that is a wonderful gift granted by the Lord Jesus Christ through the Holy Spirit. To be filled with the Holy Spirit is to be filled with the Lord Jesus Christ. Thank Him for His gift today. You might close your time with the Lord by writing a prayer in your Journal.

Rest in His Love
"But you will receive power when the Holy Spirit comes on you; and you will be my witnesses in Jerusalem, and in all Judea and Samaria, and to the ends of the earth" (Acts 1:8, NIV).

believe in Him

"He who believes in Me . . . "
JOHN 7:38

Prepare Your Heart

Both before and during the Welsh Revival, the leaders were unshakably confident that God was going to do a mighty work by His Holy Spirit. With childlike faith, the leaders took God's promises as their own and looked to Him to keep His Word. They felt that God was at work to do something extraordinary. Night after night, people could not wait to get to the revival meetings so that they could be present to see what God would do. They waited. And prayed. And believed. God was going to do something. He was going to pour out His Spirit in such a miraculously powerful way that people would be saved and changed. The center of attention was not the preacher, or the choir, or the offering. It was God. He was the One who had their attention. They didn't want to miss Him.

When you turn in that imperceptible moment from doubt to the belief that perhaps God is at work in your life, your confidence in what God says begins to build until His Word, His promises, become the biggest thing on your horizon. The cares of this world seem to shrink in light of what He says. You feel a new freedom to launch out on God's promises and dare to do mighty things in His power. Actions betray the degree of belief that resides in the heart. If you believe in the Lord Jesus, you will come to Him and drink that living water that satisfies your thirst.

As a preparation of heart for your time with the Lord today, turn to Psalm 18 and meditate on these words of David, the man after God's own heart. Note his confidence in his Lord. He was experienced in trusting the Lord and crying out to Him for everything. What are your favorite words in this psalm? Write them in your Journal as a prayer to the Lord.

READ AND STUDY GOD'S WORD

In John 7:37-38, Jesus presented belief as the condition for those rivers of water to begin to flow. Throughout His ministry, He used that word *believe*. Believing in Jesus is the grand imperative in experiencing personal spiritual revival, for the spiritual life is by faith, not by sight. Belief is not intellectual assent but an act of the will, a decision, a choice that you carry into actions. Your belief is something you do. What you say is important, but what you do is even more important. It demonstrates the belief in your heart.

Today think about what it means to believe in the Lord. Think about how important it is to the Lord that you believe in Him.

1. Read Mark 9:14-29. What kind of belief was the Lord asking for? How is that belief carried out in actions? Write your insights in the space provided.

2. Read Luke 8:4-15. In this parable, Jesus gives four different responses to His Word. Write out the types of soil, the responses, the reasons for each individual response, and the final result.

Luke 8:11-15	First Soil	Second Soil	Third Soil	Fourth Soil
Kind of Soil				
Response				
Reason for Response				
Result				

3. There was a point when Jesus made it very clear what He wanted others to believe. Read John 8:23-32. What are we to believe?

How will it be demonstrated in our life?

What is the result?

4. Read Hebrews 11:6. What do you learn about faith and belief?

5. How would you summarize what it means to believe in Jesus?

ADORE GOD IN PRAYER

O Lord, I have heard a good word inviting me to look away to Thee and be satisfied. My heart longs to respond, but sin has clouded my vision till I see Thee but dimly. Be pleased to cleanse me in Thine own precious blood, and make me inwardly pure, so that I may with unveiled eyes gaze upon Thee all the days of my earthly pilgrimage. Then shall I be prepared to behold Thee in full splendor in the day when Thou shalt appear to be glorified in Thy saints and admired in all them that believe. Amen.[1]

A. W. TOZER IN *THE PURSUIT OF GOD*

YIELD YOURSELF TO GOD

Believing God is just looking to God and what He is, allowing Him to reveal His presence, giving Him time and yielding the whole being to take in the full impression of what He is as God, the soul opened up to receive and rejoice in the overshadowing of His love. Yes, faith is the eye to which God shows what He is and does; through faith the light of His presence and the workings of His mighty power stream into the soul.[2]

ANDREW MURRAY IN *WITH CHRIST IN THE SCHOOL OF PRAYER*

I do beg of you to recognize, then, the extreme simplicity of faith; namely that it is nothing more nor less than just believing God when He says He either has done something for us, or will do it; and then trusting Him to keep His word. It is so simple that it is hard to explain. If anyone asks me what it means to trust another to do a piece of work for me, I can answer only that it means committing the work to that other, and leaving it without anxiety in His hands. . . . You have trusted Him in a few things, and He has not failed you. Trust Him now for everything, and see if He does not do for you exceeding abundantly, above all that you could ever have asked or even thought, not according to your power or capacity, but according to His own mighty power, working in you all the good pleasure of His most blessed will. . . . Take your stand on the trustworthiness of your God, and see how quickly all difficulties will vanish before a steadfast determination to believe. Trust in the dark, trust in the light, trust at night and trust in the morning, and you will find that the faith that many begin perhaps by a mighty effort will end, sooner or later, by becoming the easy and natural habit of the soul. It is a law of the spiritual life that every act of trust makes the next act less difficult, until at length, if these acts are persisted in, trusting becomes, like breathing, the natural unconscious action of the redeemed soul.

HANNAH WHITALL SMITH IN *THE CHRISTIAN'S SECRET OF A HAPPY LIFE*

ENJOY HIS PRESENCE

Do you believe in Jesus more than you believe in the things of this world? Does your life demonstrate it? Do you come to Him and drink in every situation of life? Do you believe He is the Resource beyond all resources? This is so important to think about as you prepare to plumb the depths of God's Word and learn about personal spiritual revival. It is imperative that you resolve to choose Jesus above the things of this world. He must be the center of attention in your life. He longs to be included at every turn of your life. Oh that we might all fix our eyes on Jesus today.

REST IN HIS LOVE

"Therefore, since we are surrounded by such a great cloud of witnesses, let us throw off everything that hinders and the sin that so easily entangles, and let us run with perseverance the race marked out for us. Let us fix our eyes on Jesus, the author and perfecter of our faith, who for the joy set before him endured the cross, scorning its shame, and sat down at the right hand of the throne of God. Consider him who endured such opposition from sinful men, so that you will not grow weary and lose heart" (Hebrews 12:1-3, NIV).

true revival: rivers of living water

"From his innermost being will flow rivers of living water."
JOHN 7:38

Prepare Your Heart

And now there is the promise of personal spiritual revival from the Lord Jesus Christ. What a phenomenal promise this is! What does Jesus promise? An abundant life. A victorious life. A vibrant life. A joyful life. A fruitful life. An overflowing life. A life filled with meaning and purpose. But the Lord is perfectly clear. It is a life that flows from within. Its origin is not outside, in the world. It is an inner life that comes from the Holy Spirit within. It is not dependent on outward circumstance but on the Lord Jesus Christ who lives in you. And the quality of life? Imagine, not just a trickle from within, but rivers of living water. That is an abundant life. And the Lord intends that you experience that life with Him in this world. What will it involve? That is what this study is all about.

Several years before Seth Joshua began preaching in Wales, God told him to pray that He would raise up a young man from the coal mines to revive His work. Corporate revival always begins with individuals who experience personal spiritual revival as part of their normal Christian lives. Evan Roberts, that young miner, had been praying for revival in Wales from age thirteen to age twenty-six. He wanted to honor God in every area of his life. He had an overwhelming sense of God's presence. In 1904, Roberts sensed that the Holy Spirit was preparing his heart for something.

Meetings began in Blaenannerch. On the second day, Seth Joshua closed the meeting in prayer, asking God to have mercy upon them and make them submissive to His will. He ended his prayer with "O Lord, bend us." Those words burned in Roberts's heart. He could not stop thinking about what Joshua had prayed. As the meeting resumed after breakfast, under the power of the Holy Spirit, Roberts fell to his knees in tears. He pleaded with God to bend him to His will. The necessity of salvation for the soul so impressed his heart that

Roberts said he "felt ablaze with a desire to go through the length and breadth of Wales to tell of the Savior." Roberts felt his life was no longer his own, but it belonged to God. And he was ready to go wherever God called him.

Roberts was also filled with a desire to spend time with God—not just minutes, but hours in Bible study, prayer, and worship. Time passed so quickly that the hours with God seemed like brief moments. In the next few weeks, the outpouring of God's Spirit began throughout Wales, one meeting after another. As Roberts moved from town to town throughout Wales, conducting meetings, the Holy Spirit moved in the hearts of men and women, bringing them to confession and repentance, salvation, and a commitment to follow Christ.

Roberts would reason with the people in an unorthodox way. There was none of the slick presentation. He would walk up and down the aisles with an open Bible in his hand, exhorting and encouraging some, kneeling in prayer with others. Someone would stand and sing. Then someone would read Scripture. The same things, characteristic of God at work, happened across Wales. The rivers of living water made their way all across that land. But they first had made their way into the hearts of individuals such as Seth Joshua and Evan Roberts.

Jesus Christ is the same yesterday, today, and forever. May those rivers of living water once again flow from your innermost being. In preparation for your time with the Lord, write a prayer in your Journal thanking Him for what He has shown you this week. Then spend a few moments communing with your Lord, with your eyes on Him only. As you turn your eyes on Him, the things of this world will grow dim. Then your heart will be prepared to hear His words.

READ AND STUDY GOD'S WORD

1. When Jesus says that "from your innermost being will flow rivers of living water," He is describing an extraordinary kind of life. It is not something a human being, a company, or a nation can manufacture. The source of this supernatural life is found in the Lord Himself. Take some time with the following verses and think about what they mean for your own life. Record your response to these words as though they were a personal invitation to you (and indeed they are).

   John 10:10

   John 15:5

Matthew 11:28-30

Isaiah 58:11

2. What is your favorite phrase in these verses?

ADORE GOD IN PRAYER

What is pressing in on your heart and life today? Turn to the Prayer Pages at the back of this book and write out the requests of your heart. Be certain to date your requests and write them out so you can see how the Lord answers your prayers.

YIELD YOURSELF TO GOD

When the fulness begins to flow out, then you realize what you could not realise before — a deeper joy, a clearer vision, greater power and more courage.[1]

EVAN HOPKINS IN *KESWICK'S AUTHENTIC VOICE*

Is your life comparable to a river, nay, to many rivers of holy influence? In the first place, do you know what it is to be satisfied? And in the second place, do you know what it is to communicate to others what you are receiving from the risen Lord? If not, are you not living below your privileges, and would it not be wise to do what the present writer did on one memorable occasion — put your finger on these words, and claim that, in all their heights, and depths, and widths, and lengths of meaning, they should be realized? The world would soon cease to be thirsty if only each believer were to become like one of the ancient rivers of Paradise, which was parted into four heads.[2]

F. B. MEYER IN *GOSPEL OF JOHN*

Enjoy His Presence

Think about the promise of living waters, where your heart is like a well-watered garden. In that garden you will meet with your Lord to commune with Him. At the end of this first week of thinking about the revival of your own heart, you might begin to pray throughout the day, *Revive my heart, O Lord.*

Rest in His Love

"And the LORD will continually guide you, and satisfy your desire in scorched places, and give strength to your bones; and you will be like a watered garden, and like a spring of water whose waters do not fail" (Isaiah 58:11).

DEAR FRIEND,

The next two days are your opportunity to review what you have learned this week. You may wish to write your thoughts and insights in your Journal. As you think about the words of Jesus in John 7:37-39, write down:

Your most significant insight:

Your favorite quote:

Your favorite verse:

This, then is the sum of the whole matter. When weary, thirsty souls go to Jesus, He gives them instant relief, by giving them His Holy Spirit; and in that most blessed of all gifts, He Himself glides into the eager nature. He does not strive nor cry; there is no sound as of a rushing storm of wind, no coronet of flame; whilst men are watching at the front door to welcome Him with blare of trumpet, He steals in at the rear, unnoticed; but, in any case, He suddenly comes to His temple, and sits in its inner shrine as a refiner and purifier of the sons of Levi. Jesus Himself is the supply of our spirits, through the Holy Ghost, whom He gives to be within us and with us for ever.[1]

F. B. MEYER IN GOSPEL OF JOHN

the pattern of revival

week
two

2 CHRONICLES 7:14

surprised by God

"If my people, who are called by my name . . . "
2 CHRONICLES 7:14 (NIV)

Prepare Your Heart

A young girl began praying for her brother's salvation. She had made the decision that she would pray for his conversion every day until it happened. One day, their mother was with some friends. She became so burdened for her son that she left the gathering, drew near to the Lord, and began pleading with God for his salvation. At the very same moment, her son was at home alone. Desiring something to read as entertainment, he looked through his father's books. One in particular caught his eye. He began reading. He came to a statement that caught his attention: "the finished work of Christ." He thought about what that meant. He realized that the debt for his sin was completely paid and that there was nothing more he could do. He fell on his knees and received Christ as his personal Savior and Lord. This young man, J. Hudson Taylor, went on to begin the China Inland Mission and draw thousands to Jesus Christ. You can read about his life in the classic *Hudson Taylor's Spiritual Secret*.[1] Hudson Taylor lived for Jesus Christ.

This week you will meditate on one of the great revival verses in God's Word in order to understand the pattern of revival in your own life. How does personal spiritual revival occur? Second Chronicles 7:14 gives the definitive word on what God is looking for. It gives you a glimpse into the Father's heart and shows you what moves Him.

After David reigned as God's king over Israel, his son Solomon became king. During Solomon's reign, the temple was built. This was a high time in Israel. Things were never better. As he dedicated the temple, Solomon prayed an important prayer to God, asking that no matter what happened in their lives, God would hear from heaven and forgive their sins. Solomon was asking whether God's people could still enjoy life with Him, even in dark times. Perhaps you wonder the same thing. When life seems impossible, can your relationship with God make a difference?

Your circumstance, your need, is the very platform for God's reviving work in your heart. As you begin your time with the Lord today, meditate on the words of Isaiah 41:17-20. Think about the difference God can make in your life. Draw near to the Lord today and pray, *Revive my heart, O Lord.*

READ AND STUDY GOD'S WORD

1. This week you will spend extended time in one of the greatest verses in the Bible: 2 Chronicles 7:14. For background, turn to 2 Chronicles 6:12–7:10. Read Solomon's prayer and the events that followed. Write out, word for word, those portions of his prayer that are significant to you today.

2. What difference do you think it made to God's people to see their leader offer a prayer like the one Solomon made to God?

3. How did God respond to Solomon's prayer? He came to Solomon in private at night. That is very important. God came not to the people corporately with His answer, but to one person. That is how revival begins. God comes to one person who has an open ear to Him. One person who longs deeply for God. One person who will intercede on behalf of a family, a neighbor, a child, a nation, a world. One person who will, day by day, open the pages of his or her Bible to hear and respond to what God has to say. That is how revival begins. You might call it *the surprise of God* as He comes face to face with you, His child, to speak to your heart through His Word. That is what happened to Solomon that night. Read 2 Chronicles 7:11-22, paying special attention to verses 13 and 14. As you read these words from God, what do you notice about His character and ways?

4. What is the word from God on how people may be revived? Write out, word for word, the text of 2 Chronicles 7:14.

5. What does it mean that you are God's person, called by His name? It means that God treasures you. When God shows you this truth in His Word, it usually seems to come as a special surprise, just when you needed to know it. Look at the following verses and record how much you mean to the Lord. Be sure to personalize each of your insights (for example, "The Lord will not forget *me*").

    Isaiah 49:15-16

    Jeremiah 31:1-4

    Zechariah 2:7-8

    John 15:13

ADORE GOD IN PRAYER

As you have studied today, what prayer has been prompted in your heart? Write out that prayer in your Journal or on a three-by-five card so you can think about it throughout the day. Thank the Lord for His presence, His love, and His work of revival in your heart.

YIELD YOURSELF TO GOD

John Piper speaks of God's great pleasure in His people in his book *The Pleasures of God.* He quotes Zephaniah 3:17: "The LORD, your God, is in your midst, a warrior who gives victory; he will rejoice over you with gladness, he will be quiet in his love; he will exult over you with loud singing." Then he talks about what it must be like to hear God singing about us. Here is what he says:

> When I hear this singing I stand dumbfounded, staggered, speechless that he is singing over me—one who has dishonored him so many times and in so many ways. It is almost too good to be true. He is rejoicing over my good with all his heart and with all his soul. He virtually breaks forth into song when he hits upon a new way to do me good.[2]

What is your view of God? Do you realize how much He loves you and wants to revive you today?

ENJOY HIS PRESENCE

In what ways has God broken through the walls of your life and surprised you? What verses from His Word have meant the most to you today?

REST IN HIS LOVE

"The afflicted and needy are seeking water, but there is none, and their tongue is parched with thirst; I, the LORD, will answer them Myself; as the God of Israel I will not forsake them" (Isaiah 41:17).

responding from the heart

" . . . will humble themselves . . . "
2 CHRONICLES 7:14

Prepare Your Heart

Personal revival begins with God. It continues with your intentional response. God revives the humble heart. He is looking for one who is absolutely dependent upon Him, overwhelmed with a sense of personal need, yielding to Him the right to be right, and sensing a need for a fresh encounter with God. The Lord loves it when, upon realizing your need, you run to Him. He loves it when you fall at His feet at the realization of your own weakness and sin. He loves it when you recognize who He is and worship Him. He is God. Your humility is a living reflection of the Lord Jesus in you because the Lord's heart is a humble heart. Out of love and obedience to His Father, He laid aside His own rights in order to be made in the likeness of man and to take the form of a bondservant. The humble heart turns to God. The humble heart is touched and changed by God.

This is what God was saying when He appeared to Solomon that night. He was saying that you are His beloved, called by His name. Humble yourself. Don't be afraid to choose the low place. Don't be afraid to seem unimportant in the eyes of people. Choose to be famous in the secret audience of God. Don't worry if it seems life is passing you by. Stay at the feet of the Lord Jesus Christ, worshiping and following Him. God has a plan. "It is God who is at work in you both to will and to work for His good pleasure" (Philippians 2:13). God wants to do something only He can do in your life. How will you respond to Him today?

As you begin your time with the Lord today, make these words be the prayer of your heart:

Draw me nearer, nearer, blessed Lord,
to the cross where thou hast died.

Draw me nearer, nearer, nearer, blessed Lord,
to thy precious, bleeding side.

FANNY CROSBY (1820–1915)

READ AND STUDY GOD'S WORD

What would you do if you knew that tomorrow morning you would awaken and within a few hours, the skies would be rolled back as a scroll, the trumpet would sound, and you would stand face to face with your Lord? How would that change your pursuits in life? How would it change how you serve at your church and in your ministry? How would it change your relationships? And how would it change your relationship with the Lord right now?

God longs for His people to turn to Him. What will it take? Realizing who God really is and who you are in the light of His presence. He is God. You are His child, created by Him to know and love Him. The only place to stand is on the ground of humility as a recipient of God's grace and mercy in the name of Jesus Christ. This is the path to ongoing personal spiritual revival. When you walk that path, you will discover that you are standing on holy ground.

1. Humility occurs when one is faced with the true character and ways of God as seen in His Word. It is the only response to a view of your almighty God. Consider Job, for example. Few have suffered as much as he. He wrestled with life's questions. He said many things to his friends and to God. It was only when he saw and heard from God that he had nothing to say. Read Job's response to God in Job 42:1-6. What do you see in his words that helps you understand what it means to humble yourself?

2. Read these verses from some of the Old Testament prophets. At this time, God's people were disobeying and suffering the consequences described in 2 Chronicles 6:22-39. What does God think when His people refuse to turn to Him? What does He want from them? Look for any insights that will help you understand how you can humble yourself before the Lord.

Isaiah 65:1-7

Jeremiah 2:1-19,32

Jeremiah 8:4-9

Joel 2:12-14

3. Summarize what you see in these verses that helps you understand what it means to humble yourself before the Lord when He speaks.

4. What is God's promise of revival in Isaiah 57:15-16?

5. What is His promise in Acts 3:19?

ADORE GOD IN PRAYER

Are you willing to humble yourself before the Lord and allow Him to make you the person He wants you to be? Is there any area of your life where you are trying to exalt yourself, be self-sufficient, or gain applause from others? Is there any situation where you are holding on to the right to be right? Can you lay that aside? Draw near to the Lord today and lay yourself at His feet. Place all that you are in His hands. Humility is the beauty of holiness, according to Andrew Murray. You are most beautiful in the eyes of the Lord when you reflect the humility of Jesus Christ.

YIELD YOURSELF TO GOD

Heart-rending is divinely wrought and solemnly felt. It is a secret grief which is personally experienced, not in mere form, but as a deep, soul-moving work of the Holy Spirit upon the inmost heart of each believer. It is not a matter to be merely talked of and believed in, but keenly and sensitively felt in every living child of the living God. It is powerfully humiliating, and completely sin-purging; but then it is sweetly preparative for those gracious consolations which proud unhumbled spirits are unable to receive; and it is distinctly discriminating, for it belongs to the elect of God, and to them alone.[1]

CHARLES SPURGEON IN MORNING AND EVENING

The self-centred life loves to be noticed by others. It loves the praise of men, and is evidently delighted when it is the sole object of admiration. It loves the highest place and draws attention to itself perpetually in one way or another. The self-centered Christian looks for opportunities to tell others of what he has done for the Lord — perhaps in a very pious way but secretly expecting their appreciation. And he is very unhappy and uneasy when someone else succeeds or has done something better than himself. . . . The self-centered Christian does not know how to take the second place graciously and joyfully. He is upset when someone else is given the leadership and he himself has to play second fiddle. . . . A self-centered Christian leader hinders others below him from becoming leaders, lest his own position be threatened. And so he ministers in such a way as to make himself a necessity to those to whom he ministers. . . . No one is indispensable in Christ's Church. God's work can easily carry on without us. In fact, it can carry on much better without the help of those conceited folk who consider themselves indispensable! We must recognize this fact constantly. And so, we must be willing to withdraw into the background anytime God calls us to. But the self-centered Christian worker will never accept that. He will want to hold on to his position for as long as possible. Many such "Christian leaders" are rotting on their "thrones" today hindering the work of God. They do not know what it is to fade graciously into the background and let someone else take their place.[2]

ZAC POONEN IN *BEAUTY FOR ASHES*

Let us learn the lesson: the highest holiness is the deepest humility; and let us remember that it comes not of itself, but only as it is made a matter of special dealing on the part of our faithful Lord and His faithful servant. . . . It is indeed blessed, the deep happiness of heaven, to be so free from self that whatever is said of us or done to us is lost and swallowed up in the thought that Jesus is all.[3]

ANDREW MURRAY IN *HUMILITY*

ENJOY HIS PRESENCE

Come Lord, and abide with me. Come, and occupy alone the throne of my heart; reign there without a rival, and consecrate me entirely to Thy service.[4]

CHARLES SPURGEON IN *MORNING AND EVENING*

REST IN HIS LOVE

"'Return to Me with all your heart, and with fasting, weeping and mourning; and rend your heart and not your garments.' Now return to the LORD your God, for He is gracious and compassionate, slow to anger, abounding in lovingkindness and relenting of evil" (Joel 2:12-13).

the pursuit of God

" . . . pray and seek My face. . . "
2 CHRONICLES 7:14

Prepare Your Heart

The great men and women of God through the centuries have possessed one common quality. They had hearts that beat for God and were filled with a passionate desire to know and love Him. In a practical way, day by day, they paid the price in time and energy to know the Lord. They developed a rich quiet time with the Lord. They set aside time and a place to meet with Him in His Word and in prayer. That is what it means to pray and seek His face. Quiet time with the Lord is not a complicated mystery. It is simply developing an intimate relationship with God. And it is not something that just happens. It is intentional. There is a learning curve that involves time and energy.

How can you learn to spend time with God? First, it is important that you study some of the great ones in the Christian life. Some of the best are A. W. Tozer (*The Pursuit of God* and *The Knowledge of the Holy*), Oswald Chambers (*My Utmost for His Highest*), and Amy Carmichael (*The Edges of His Ways* and *Thou Givest, They Gather*). Other classic devotional writers are Andrew Murray, G. Campbell Morgan, J. I. Packer (*Knowing God*), Charles Spurgeon, Alan Redpath (*The Making of a Man of God*), Elisabeth Elliot (*The Shadow of the Almighty*), R. A. Torrey, and E. M. Bounds. All of these writers will help you learn what it is to draw near to God. They will challenge you to go deep with God and never compromise in your relationship with Him.

To grow in your quiet time, it is important to develop friendships with those who are also committed to knowing God. Those people are few and far between. There are so many in the church today who are dabblers. A little bit here, a little bit there. Every now and then, you will find those rare friends who have engaged in the pursuit of God. They are the ones who are experiencing the great adventure of knowing God. And they will be the ones to challenge you to grow in your quiet time with God. They will ask you, "What is God teaching you?" You need friends like that.

Don't be afraid to try new things in your quiet time. You will discover, as you spend time with God, that He will bring ideas to your mind, such as writing out Scripture in your Journal or praying His Word back to Him. This book of quiet times is designed to help you develop your quiet time with God by actually spending time with Him. The best way to develop a quiet time with the Lord is to actually do it. Day by day, pay the price by sitting down with the Lord and spending time with Him. That is how you will grow in your quiet time. If you do this, your quiet time will become like second nature to you, and God will use you to challenge others who are just beginning the adventure.

Developing your quiet time is a great secret to personal spiritual revival. The quiet place alone with God is where He meets with you, speaks to you in His Word, and makes you the person He wants you to be.

As a preparation of heart today, meditate on Psalm 105:1-5. Then write a prayer, asking the Lord to teach you how to pray and seek His face. Ask Him to enrich your quiet time.

READ AND STUDY GOD'S WORD

The Old Testament is a lesson in the difference that seeking God's face makes in the direction and influence of a life. Today you will look at two kings: King Asa and his son Jehoshaphat.

1. Turn to 2 Chronicles 14–16 and read about the life of King Asa. How did he live? Where did he go wrong? Record your insights.

2. Read 2 Chronicles 17:1-6. What do you see in the life of Jehoshaphat that will help you in your own life?

3. Look at the following verses and record what you learn about seeking the Lord.
2 Chronicles 12:13-14

Psalm 34:10

Isaiah 55:6

Amos 5:6

4. Meditate on James 4:8. What difference do you think it makes in life if you choose to draw near to God?

ADORE GOD IN PRAYER

Lord Jesus, I thank you that a new day affords another opportunity for consecration and devotion. You have turned a fresh page in my life's story. It comes from you without blemish or soil; help me to keep it so. Forgive the past blotted with failures and sins, and help me to walk in the light.[1]

F. B. MEYER IN *DAILY PRAYERS*

YIELD YOURSELF TO GOD

It would be well if the dwellers in the valley could frequently leave their abodes among the marshes and fever mists, and inhale the bracing element upon the hills. It is to such an exploit of climbing that I invite you this evening. May the Spirit of God assist us to leave the mists of fear and the fevers of anxiety, and all the ills which gather in this valley of earth, and to ascend the mountains of anticipated joys and blessedness. May God the Holy Spirit cut the cords that keep us here below, and assist us to the mount! We sit too often like chained eagles fastened to the rock, only that, unlike the eagle, we begin to love our chain, and would, perhaps, if it came really to the test, be loath to have it snapped. May God now grant us grace, if we cannot escape from the chain as to our flesh, yet to do so as to our spirits; and leaving the body like a servant, at the foot of the hill, may our soul, like Abraham, attain the top of the mountain, there to indulge in communion with the Most High.[2]

CHARLES SPURGEON IN *MORNING AND EVENING*

As we begin to focus upon God, the things of the spirit will take shape before our inner eyes. Obedience to the word of Christ will bring an inward revelation of the Godhead (John 14:21-23). It will give acute perception enabling us to see God even as is promised to the pure in heart. A new God-consciousness will seize upon us and we shall begin to taste and hear and inwardly feel God, who is our life and our all. There will be seen the constant shining of *the true Light, which lighteth every man that cometh into the world* (John 1:9). More and more, as our faculties grow sharper and more sure, God will become to us the great All, and His presence the glory and wonder of our lives.[3]

A. W. TOZER IN *THE PURSUIT OF GOD*

ENJOY HIS PRESENCE
Every day you are faced with a choice. Will you say no to some good things in order to carve out some daily time alone with God where you can pray and seek His face? This is vital if you desire to be personally, spiritually revived.

REST IN HIS LOVE
"You will seek Me and find Me when you search for Me with all your heart" (Jeremiah 29:13).

living out the Word

" . . . turn from their wicked ways . . . "
2 CHRONICLES 7:14

Prepare Your Heart

God always expects action when He speaks in His Word. In the case of His words to Solomon, He required a *turn* from *wicked ways*. That word *turn* in the Hebrew implies a turning away from sin in such a way that a person returns to God and His will for his or her life.[1]

God never sends out His Word without a purpose of transformation. He says,

"For as the rain and the snow come down from heaven, and do not return there without watering the earth and making it bear and sprout, and furnishing seed to the sower and bread to the eater; so will My word be which goes forth from My mouth; it will not return to Me empty, without accomplishing what I desire, and without succeeding in the matter for which I sent it." (Isaiah 55:10-11)

These are powerful words. Today, as you begin your time with the Lord, meditate on them and think about what they mean for your life. Thank the Lord for the wondrous gift of His Word today.

READ AND STUDY GOD'S WORD

King Ahaz was one who did not do right in the sight of the Lord as David his father had done (see 2 Chronicles 28:1). In fact, near the end of his life, in the time of his distress, this same king became yet more unfaithful to the Lord (see 2 Chronicles 28:22). Ahaz made a bad decision. The decisions that many people consider trivial are sometimes the ones where life hangs in the balance.

Choosing to follow the Lord, day after day, is the most important decision one can ever make. Actions flow out of the convictions and resolve that are developed in your quiet time with God. The Word of God is given that you might live it out. James makes it clear:

Therefore, putting aside all filthiness and all that remains of wickedness, in humility receive the word implanted, which is able to save your souls. But prove yourselves doers of the word, and not merely hearers who delude themselves. For if anyone is a hearer of the word and not a doer, he is like a man who looks at his natural face in a mirror; for once he has looked at himself and gone away, he has immediately forgotten what kind of person he was. But one who looks intently at the perfect law, the law of liberty, and abides by it, not having become a forgetful hearer but an effectual doer, this man will be blessed in what he does. (James 1:21-25)

1. After the reign of Ahaz, Hezekiah became king at the age of twenty-five. Hezekiah's actions and the actions of those who served under him illustrate what can happen when we carry out what God shows us in our quiet times. Turn to 2 Chronicles 29. Record everything Hezekiah and his people did.

2. Read 2 Chronicles 30–31. What did Hezekiah do?

3. What effect did Hezekiah's actions have on his people?

4. How can the actions of one believer who does God's will as revealed in His Word make a difference in the lives of others?

ADORE GOD IN PRAYER

Lord, make me childlike. Deliver me from the urge to compete with another for place or prestige or position. I would be simple and artless as a little child. Deliver me from pose and pretense. Forgive me for thinking of myself. Help me to forget myself and find my true peace in beholding Thee. That Thou mayest answer this prayer I humble myself before Thee. Lay upon me Thy easy yoke of Self Forgetfulness that through it I may find rest. Amen.[2]

A. W. TOZER IN THE PURSUIT OF GOD

YIELD YOURSELF TO GOD

Your words were found and I ate them, and Your words became for me a joy and the delight of my heart; for I have been called by Your name, O LORD God of hosts.

JEREMIAH 15:16

Taking a small portion of God's Word, some definite command or duty of the new life, quietly receiving it into the will and the love of the heart, yielding the whole being to its rule, and vowing, in the power of the Lord Jesus, to perform it. This, and then going to do it, this is eating the Word, taking it so into our innermost being that it becomes a constituent part of our very life. The same with a truth, or a promise; what you have eaten now becomes part of yourself; you carry it with you where you go as part of the life you live.[3]

ANDREW MURRAY IN THE INNER LIFE

ENJOY HIS PRESENCE

What is God asking you to do today? How can you live in such a way that those around you will be drawn to Jesus Christ? Can you see the need for beginning and maintaining a life of consecration? Is there a sin you need to confess, an activity you need to lay aside, a relationship that needs to be repaired, or a ministry you need to begin? Will you be like Hezekiah today and begin and maintain a life that is totally devoted to the Lord Jesus Christ? Think about the difference Hezekiah made in the lives of his people. And think about the difference that one person who is totally sold out for the sake of Christ can make in his or her generation.

REST IN HIS LOVE

"There will be more joy in heaven over one sinner who repents than over ninety-nine righteous persons who need no repentance" (Luke 15:7).

God hears, God revives

" . . . then will I hear from heaven and will forgive their sin and will heal their land."
2 CHRONICLES 7:14 (NIV)

Prepare Your Heart

Revival is receiving from God the restoration and strength that you need in order to walk with Him. He gives you what you need to carry on. It may come in the form of forgiveness of sin, strength in weakness, a change in attitude, love for an enemy, an idea for ministry, or wisdom in a difficult situation. Whenever the Lord works in your heart and in your life, you are experiencing His reviving touch through the power of the Holy Spirit. This is why personal revival must be seen as absolutely necessary to your normal experience with God. It is not something elusive and optional. It is vital.

Corporate revival is something God does in response to His people's prayers at special times and places, according to His will. And corporate revival always begins with those who know personal revival as part of their relationships with God. God may choose to use you as one of those who, like Evan Roberts in the Welsh Revival, will be a catalyst for widespread revival throughout the world. Today, as you think about God's reviving touch in your own life, ask God to open your eyes to behold wonderful things from His Word. Begin your time today by praying, *Revive my heart, O Lord.*

READ AND STUDY GOD'S WORD

God longs to revive people and restore them to the true purpose that He has ordained for them. Then God is glorified and those He loves experience His blessing. The city of Nineveh is an example of God's heart for revival. God used a man named Jonah to preach the Word to this city, and because the Ninevites responded to God, the course of their lives changed.

Nineveh was the capital of Assyria, and its people were idol worshipers with a reputation for brutality, yet God longed for their repentance. The same thing can happen to us. When we respond to God's Word in humility, in wholehearted pursuit of God and repentance of our own ways, God hears and God revives.

1. Turn to Jonah 3. Record the message God brought to Nineveh through Jonah. Then record how the Ninevites responded. Finally, record God's activity in relation to their response.

The Message	Nineveh's Response	God's Activity

2. How do you think the lives of those in Nineveh changed as a result of God's message?

3. Look at the following verses and record how God works in your life to make a difference.

John 15:11

Galatians 5:22-24

Philippians 2:13

Romans 5:3-5

Romans 12:1-2

4. How can God's work of revival make a difference in your own life?

ADORE GOD IN PRAYER

Meditate on the words of this hymn by William P. Mackay:

> Revive us again—fill each heart with Thy love;
> May each soul be rekindled with fire from above.
> Hallelujah, Thine the glory! Hallelujah, amen!
> Hallelujah, Thine the glory! Revive us again.

YIELD YOURSELF TO GOD

Revival comes through obedience. Indeed revival is really just obeying the Holy Ghost. Where He tells us to "break" and to testify to the light shining on sin in our lives, and on the blood which cleanses from all sin, then let us obey, and we will find at once that the Spirit is loosed in revival in our own hearts, and is moving in revival in the company.[1]

NORMAN GRUBB IN *CONTINUOUS REVIVAL*

Deeper even than the outward signs, however, is the transaction about which the world knows nothing (although it will see evidence of its reality in his life) that comes when he lifts up his face to the Lord Jesus and says, "Lord, I'm not interested in Your blessings; all I want is that You should reign in peace in Your own house. Let them take all the material things, Lord. But I am Your property; my body is the temple of the Holy Spirit. I am Your blood-bought child, Lord Jesus, and therefore I belong to You completely." Do you see it, friend? Oh, how poverty-stricken are words to speak on such a subject! Are you in the condition which grace meets? Then think about the salvation which grace ministers to you: you are accepted by virtue of the blood of the cross, because of what He has done for you. That truth brings you in abasement to the foot of the cross, and because you come like that, there is ministered to you the abundance of God's salvation. Then there comes the response which grace merits from your life—an abstinence from the world, and abandonment to God in Jesus Christ which enables you to say with the Apostle Paul, *But God forbid that I should glory, save in the cross of our Lord Jesus Christ, by whom the world is crucified unto me, and I unto the world* (Galatians 6:14).[2]

ALAN REDPATH IN *THE MAKING OF A MAN OF GOD*

ENJOY HIS PRESENCE

How will you respond to God's Word today? Will you be personally, spiritually revived by Him?

REST IN HIS LOVE

"For thus says the high and exalted One who lives forever, whose name is Holy, 'I dwell on a high and holy place, and also with the contrite and lowly of spirit in order to revive the spirit of the lowly and to revive the heart of the contrite'" (Isaiah 57:15).

Dear Friend,

This week you have seen the pattern of personal spiritual revival. Understanding it will lead more and more to the actual desire and experience of it. Summarize in two to three sentences your understanding of the pattern of revival from your study this week.

What were your most meaningful discoveries this week as you spent time with the Lord?
Most meaningful insight:

Most meaningful devotional reading:

Most meaningful verse:

Are you satisfied with the condition of the Church? Are you satisfied with your own condition? You, who believe the truth, you who are evangelical, you who are not a liberal in your theology. That is good, but is that enough? What is our spiritual state and condition in reality? How do we feel when we read the experiences of these apostles, the Apostle Paul and others? Can we say honestly, with him, that we are in a kind of state of tension, saying *That I may know him, and the power of his resurrection, and the fellowship of his sufferings . . . not as though I had already attained . . . forgetting those things which are behind . . . I press toward* (Philippians 3:10-14)? Do you feel the tension, the concern, the stretching, the pressing on? How much do we know of that? Can we honestly say that we rejoice in the Lord Jesus Christ with *a joy unspeakable and full of glory?* Can we say with Paul that to us *to live is Christ, and to die is gain?* That we might *be with Christ, which is far better. . . .* Now these are the ways in which we are to test ourselves. There is no hope for true prayer and intercession for revival unless we realize that there is a need. Is all well with us? Can we be satisfied? Can we sit back and fold our arms and say "Things are going marvelously, look at the reports." Are we like the Israelites at this point, or are we like the Laodiceans saying that we are rich, that we have abundance, that all is well with us, and failing to realize that we are poor and wretched and blind? May God give us grace to examine ourselves, and be honest with ourselves. . . . My dear friends, the first step is that you and I have to realize these things. We have to be pulled up by them, to begin to think about them, to become concerned about them and have a deep awareness of the position as it is.[1]

D. Martyn Lloyd-Jones in Revival

the need for revival

week
three

PSALM 119

like a wineskin in the smoke

Though I have become like a wineskin in the smoke,
I do not forget Your statutes.
PSALM 119:83

Prepare Your Heart

On October 24, 1931, Amy Carmichael was checking out some property for her mission-ary work. As she walked across the land, she fell and was badly injured. That brief moment changed her life. She spent the next twenty years bedridden with constant pain. It was certainly not what she had in mind when she prayed earlier in the day, "Do with me as Thou wilt. Do anything, Lord, that will fit me to serve Thee and help my beloveds."[1] Yet those were not idle words. Amy had a heart for the Lord. She was seasoned in drawing near to Him daily for everything she needed. She lived in God's Word. And when the storm came, she discovered that she had resources from her Lord that would sustain her even in the dark-est of times.

Those last twenty years of her life proved to be her most productive. She wrote thirteen books, and many of her older books were republished. The Lord was Amy's source of strength and encouragement. As a result, she experienced the personal spiritual revival that comes from knowing and believing in the Lord Jesus Christ.

As you begin this study on personal spiritual revival, take some time to draw near to the Lord. Ask Him to give you a willing heart and a teachable spirit. Turn to Psalm 63, and medi-tate on the words of David. Choose the one verse that is most significant to you, and use it to write a prayer to the Lord.

READ AND STUDY GOD'S WORD

The main passage for our study on personal revival is Psalm 119. Psalm 119 is the longest
psalm in the Bible. Except for four verses, the entire psalm is addressed directly to God.
Whenever you study a passage in Scripture, you need to understand its background. The
Psalms often begin with a superscription that identifies the author. In the case of Psalm 119,
there is no superscription. The best way to understand the author and his situation is to read
the psalm. For the next two days, you will have the opportunity to do that. You will discover
that the author of this psalm was a godly man in great need of personal revival.

   1. Read Psalm 119:1-88, looking for clues to the life, character, and circumstances of the
author. Look for personal pronouns, such as *I*, *me*, or *my*. You may wish to underline or
circle each occurrence in your Bible. You will want a Bible with enough space in the mar-
gins and between lines and words that you can easily mark key words and make notations. You may wish to get a Bible that you use just for this study so you can feel free to
mark in it. Choose a translation that is easy to read, such as the *New American Standard
Updated Edition* or the *New International Version*. Record the author's desires, frustrations, and
anything you learn about his relationship to God. (If you need more space, use a journal
page in the back of this book.)

2. Summarize what you learned about the author in two or three sentences.

3. In what ways did you identify with the author?

ADORE GOD IN PRAYER

Turn to the Lord now and pray, *Revive my heart, O Lord.* You may wish to turn to the Prayer Pages in the back of this study book and record your prayer requests along with the date. Feel free to use the Prayer Pages to write out any other prayers that are on your heart.

YIELD YOURSELF TO GOD

You look back at a certain moment which changed everything. But moment is too long a word; was it a period of time at all? There came a thunder clap. But no, thunder may rumble for two or three seconds. This was a lightning-flash cleaving straight across the road on which you walked. You shut your eyes instinctively; when you opened them the road looked different. And it was different. Nothing will ever be again as it was before that lightning-flash. This, and this, and this you will never do again. And the road will grow duller and darker with every mile you go—is that your thought?

A Voice speaks within you: "Things will never be as they were before? That is true; for they will be better. You will never do this and this again? That also is true; for I have other things for you to do. They are not what you would choose? But they are indeed the best that Love can choose for you. The road will grow duller and darker with every mile you go? The path is like a shining light; like the sun that you have watched on many a lovely morning coming out of his chambers and rejoicing as a strong man to run a race. Does the light on that shining race-course of the sky grow less and less? No, it shineth more and more. So shall the path of My beloved be, not darker, but brighter as it nears the perfect day. This is the heritage of the servants of the Lord. *This*, not that."[2]

AMY CARMICHAEL IN *GOLD BY MOONLIGHT*

No matter where you are, no matter how desperate or difficult your circumstances become, God has a plan. His plan for you includes Himself as your great treasure. The light of the world, Jesus Christ, walks with you. He, your Lord, wants to revive you in the midst of your circumstances.

ENJOY HIS PRESENCE

The author of Psalm 119 describes himself as having become "like a wineskin in the smoke" (verse 83). If a wineskin hangs over the fire long enough, it becomes black, parched, dried up, and shriveled. Have you ever felt like that? You've been in the fire so long it seems there is no hope of an answer from God. Be encouraged. There is an answer for you in the prayer of this psalmist: *Revive me, O Lord.* Your goal today is simply to hold that prayer to your heart and pray it to the Lord throughout the day.

REST IN HIS LOVE

"The afflicted and needy are seeking water, but there is none, and their tongue is parched with thirst; I, the LORD, will answer them Myself, as the God of Israel I will not forsake them. I will open rivers on the bare heights and springs in the midst of the valleys; I will make the wilderness a pool of water and the dry land fountains of water" (Isaiah 41:17-18). (If you need more space, use a journal page in the back of this book.)

astray like a lost sheep

I have gone astray like a lost sheep; seek Your servant,
For I do not forget Your commandments.
PSALM 119:176

Prepare Your Heart

Astray like a lost sheep. Those are the words of a godly man who has an incredible passion for God and His Word. Yet in the midst of a fiery trial, he feels so far from God that he has lost his bearings. Have you ever felt like that? This psalmist is a man of God, mature in his faith. All men and women of God, no matter how mature, experience afflictions that challenge them to the core of their souls. The trial seems out of place, like God would never allow something like this. Maybe that, but not this. The blow leaves one feeling astray like a lost sheep.

If you are there even now, don't think you are the only one. The greatest saints have experienced such desolation. Yet for them, the place of desolation has also been the place of glory. God is there on that holy ground, doing a mighty work in the heart of a man or woman who belongs to Him.

Amy Carmichael described a time in her ministry in India when it seemed as though the entire work would not survive. On one of the most turbulent days, the only way she and her coworkers made it through was to imagine that they were all in a little ship on the raging waters of Galilee and that Jesus was in the boat with them. As long as they knew Jesus was in the boat with them, they had the courage to wait for the calm that would come when He stilled the storm.

In what way are you in need of the soothing, comforting words of the Lord Jesus today? Draw near to Him now and ask Him to speak to your heart.

READ AND STUDY GOD'S WORD

1. Today you will continue to study the author of Psalm 119. Yesterday you discovered that he loved God and His Word and yet was experiencing tremendous affliction. Read Psalm 119:89-176 and record everything you learn about the author. Pay special attention to his feelings about God and His Word. (If you need more space, use a journal page in the back of this book.

2. Summarize in one or two sentences your most significant insights about the author of Psalm 119.

3. How would you describe the author's circumstances? What do you think he was experiencing?

4. Why was he in need of revival? Read back through your observations about him and list those things he said that made you understand that he needed revival.

ADORE GOD IN PRAYER
Read through your observations of Psalm 119. Remember that this psalm is a prayer to the Lord. Choose a verse that best describes the cry of your heart today and write it out, personalizing the words to fit your own life.

YIELD YOURSELF TO GOD

There is a place where love can be renewed. "Now there was leaning on Jesus' bosom one of His disciples whom Jesus loved . . . there stood by the Cross of Jesus the disciple whom He loved. Jesus saith, *I thirst.*"

But more than pains that racked Him then
Was the deep longing thirst Divine
That thirsted for the souls of men:
Dear Lord, and one was mine.

It was the disciple who leaned upon His breast and stood beside His Cross who heard that word, "I thirst." Is it not always so? O Lord of Calvary, hold us close to Thee that we shall be drawn into that fellowship, that thirst.

This prayer goes very deep. It is not a light thing to ask to share in the fellowship of His sufferings, which is the fellowship of His love and of His thirst. "He that is not ready to suffer all things and to stand at the will of His Beloved is not worthy to be called a lover." We know we are not worthy. Such a life is like that knowledge which is "too high for me. I cannot attain unto it." We cannot attain, but when the Most High stoops to us who are low and fills us with the power of His life, then nothing is impossible. It is not that we attain. It is that He in us does that which we could never do.[1]

AMY CARMICHAEL IN GOLD BY MOONLIGHT

ENJOY HIS PRESENCE

Today do you need what only God can do? Know that the Lord is with you. He will never leave or forsake you. When you are in that dry place, needing revival from the Lord, you may feel you are far away from God. You may feel you have done something wrong. You may feel like a lost sheep. Ask God to search and cleanse your heart so you may once again experience His smile. Perhaps you are thirsting for God because He has placed that thirst deep in your heart, that you might search Him out in a deeper way than ever before. Perhaps God wants to show you something new about Himself. God desires an intimate, open, vulnerable relationship with you. Don't be afraid. Instead, draw near. Pray that prayer that comes from deep within your heart and soul: *Revive my heart, O Lord.*

REST IN HIS LOVE

"I waited patiently for the LORD; and He inclined to me and heard my cry. He brought me up out of the pit of destruction, out of the miry clay, and He set my feet upon a rock making my footsteps firm. He put a new song in my mouth, a song of praise to our God; many will see and fear and will trust in the LORD" (Psalm 40:1-3).

o how i love your law!

O how I love Your law!
It is my meditation all the day.
PSALM 119:97

Prepare Your Heart

One man. One woman. Single-minded in goal and purpose. A passion for God and His Word. Someone like that can turn the world upside down. George Mueller was such a person. As a boy, cagey and bright, George devised ways to steal the government funds in his father's keeping. His father wanted George to be a clergyman and sent him to the Cathedral Classical School. With little supervision, Mueller played cards and frequented local taverns. While his father was out of town, Mueller would collect money owed for taxes, then spend it on himself.

At nineteen, Mueller entered Halle University as a student of Divinity. He and a friend decided to spend a month in Switzerland while their parents thought they were at school. Mueller's friend was filled with remorse and confessed what they had done to his father. He began attending a Saturday night Christian meeting. Soon Mueller asked to go to the meeting too. When he saw people on their knees praying to God, he was profoundly moved. As he walked home, he declared to his friend, "All we have seen on our journey to Switzerland, and all our former pleasures are as nothing in comparison with this evening!" George Mueller received Christ that evening. New life began.

Mueller spent six months at a London seminary, where he learned the value of meditation upon the Scriptures. This practice transformed his life and desires. The man who had once devised ways to take money was now consumed with the desire to wholeheartedly trust God to provide for his every need and then give what God gave him to others who were in need.

Three weeks after Mueller married a woman named Mary Groves, they made a heart decision to depend upon God alone to provide for their needs. They would not even give definite answers to inquiries as to whether or not they needed money at any particular moment. No matter how pressing the need, they turned to the Lord in prayer. Mueller's ministry flourished. His Scriptural Knowledge Institution For Home and Abroad matriculated over 121,000 students and distributed 300,000 Bibles, 1.5 million New Testaments, and 111 million tracts. By 1870 he had built five orphanages and, by prayer and faith in God, was feeding 2,100 orphans daily. He solicited from no one and told only the Lord of the daily needs. In response to his prayers, over his lifetime, God gave him more than anyone else who lived at that time—7.5 million dollars—which he wisely and prayerfully distributed in the spreading of the gospel.

Mueller read the Bible through over a hundred times, half of that on his knees, where he claimed the promise, "Open thy mouth wide, and I will fill it" (Psalm 81:10, KJV). His life demonstrated to an unbelieving nation that God was still in control. England was changed because of his life. While Charles Dickens was writing about orphans and outcasts, Mueller, as a servant of the Lord and with the resources of God, was providing them with homes and food.

One person, revived by God, can make a difference. Today, as you spend time with the Lord, ask Him to prepare your heart to listen to what He says in His Word.

READ AND STUDY GOD'S WORD

It is clear from the words of the author of Psalm 119 that his heart is in trouble. He is very descriptive in his feelings of emotional pain:

- "My soul cleaves to the dust" (verse 25).
- "My soul weeps because of grief" (verse 28).
- "My soul languishes for Your salvation" (verse 81).
- "I am exceedingly afflicted" (verse 107).
- "Trouble and anguish have come upon me" (verse 143).
- "I cried with all my heart" (verse 145).

In the face of enemies, his only true support was God:

- "Princes sit and talk against me" (verse 23).
- "The arrogant utterly deride me" (verse 51).
- "Burning indignation has seized me because of the wicked, who forsake Your law" (verse 53).
- "The cords of the wicked have encircled me" (verse 61).
- "The arrogant have forged a lie against me" (verse 69).
- "They subvert me with a lie" (verse 78).
- "The arrogant have dug pits for me" (verse 85).
- "They almost destroyed me on earth" (verse 87).

In spite of his affliction, he passionately loved God and His Word:

- "With all my heart I have sought You" (verse 10).
- "I have rejoiced in the way of your testimonies as much as in all riches" (verse 14).
- "My eyes fail with longing for Your Word" (verse 82).
- "I am Yours" (verse 94).
- "How sweet are Your words to my taste!" (verse 103).
- "I have inherited Your testimonies forever, for they are the joy of my heart" (verse 111).
- "I am Your servant" (verse 125).
- "Great are Your mercies, O LORD" (verse 156).

Some commentators say that Psalm 119 is simply a collection of sayings about the Word of God. However, closer examination reveals that it is a prayer written by a servant of God whose heart is in trouble and in need of personal spiritual revival. Some have thought the author to be David. Others have attributed the psalm to someone in the time after Israel's exile to Babylon, after God sent His people into captivity because of their disobedience and idolatry.

In his commentary on the Psalms, Stewart Perowne says he believes Psalm 119 was written after the exile because (1) the references to wicked "princes" and "kings" indicate foreign domination, (2) the Law was daily study for the psalmist, so the text was now "in the hands of the people," (3) the psalm is placed near the end of the collection of psalms, (4) it is more of a meditation than poetry, and (5) the acrostic structure (each section of verses begins with successive letters of the Hebrew alphabet) was not used in earlier psalms.[1]

While no one knows with certainty who the author was, there is one person described in the Bible who shared the emotion and viewpoint of Psalm 119 during the post-exilic period. That person is Ezra. Some commentators think the author could have been Ezra. If it was not him, it was someone very much like him in character and circumstances. So as we think about this psalm, let's look more closely at Ezra.

1. To understand Psalm 119 and Ezra, it is important to grasp what was going on during Ezra's life. Because of their idolatry and disobedience, the people of Israel were conquered and deported to the Babylonian Empire between 597 and 586 B.C. The temple in Jerusalem was destroyed. In about 538 B.C., the Persian king Cyrus conquered the Babylonian Empire and issued a decree to allow the Jewish people to return to Jerusalem and rebuild their temple. You can imagine what it must have been like for these people to return to their homeland and see it in utter ruin. Yet it was a time of hope and joy, a time for God to do something new. Turn to the book of Ezra in the Old Testament and read Ezra 1–6. Then briefly describe what you think it was like to be one of God's people returning to Jerusalem.

2. Read Ezra 7:1-10 and record everything you learn about Ezra.

3. What stands out the most to you about Ezra's character?

ADORE GOD IN PRAYER

What circumstances are pressing in on you today and perhaps troubling your heart? List those things on one of the Prayer Pages in the back of this book. Title your page something like, "Troubles Entrusted to God" or "Areas Where I Need Revival." Pray through those situations, leaving each in the compassionate care of your loving Lord.

YIELD YOURSELF TO GOD

The first three years after conversion, I neglected the Word of God. Since I began to search it diligently, the blessing has been wonderful. I have read the Bible through one hundred times and always with increasing delight. I look upon it as a lost day when I have not a good time over the Word of God. Friends often say "I have so much to do, so many people to see, I cannot find time for Scripture study." Perhaps there are not many who have more to do than I. For more than half a century I have never known one day when I had not more business than I could get through. For forty years I have had annually about thirty thousand letters, and most of these passed through my own hands. I have nine assistants always at work corresponding in German, French, English, Danish, Italian, Russian, and other languages. Then as pastor of a church with twelve hundred believers, great has been my care. Besides, I have had charge of five immense orphanages; also, at my publishing depot, the printing and circulating of millions of tracts, books and Bibles. But I have always make it a rule never to begin work till I have had a good season with God. The vigor of our spiritual life will be in exact proportion to the place held by the Word in our life and thoughts.

GEORGE MUELLER

ENJOY HIS PRESENCE

What place does God's Word have in your life? Ezra "set his heart to study the law of the LORD and to practice it, and to teach His statutes and ordinances in Israel" (Ezra 7:10). The writer of Psalm 119 also delighted in God's Word. Do you delight in God's Word in the same way? Begin to think about the place God's Word holds in your own life, for you are going to discover that this is one of the great keys to personal revival.

What have you learned today that has affected your life the most? Write that truth in your Journal found at the back of this book. Then carry that truth with you throughout the day.

REST IN HIS LOVE

"For the word of God is living and active and sharper than any two-edged sword, and piercing as far as the division of soul and spirit, of both joints and marrow, and able to judge the thoughts and intentions of the heart" (Hebrews 4:12).

i cried with all my heart

I cried with all my heart; answer me, O LORD!
PSALM 119:145

Prepare Your Heart

Have you ever felt as though everything seems to be going wrong? As though no one around you really loves the Lord? That you are the only one? And because you seem to be surrounded by godlessness and troubles, you find your own life of faith to be severely compromised and in danger of failing? This was the situation for the author of Psalm 119. Where did he run in his time of trouble? To the only One who had strength and power to deal with his situation: the Lord, the Creator of the universe. As you draw near to the Lord today, ask Him to speak to you in His Word.

READ AND STUDY GOD'S WORD

Ezra was a committed man of God in the midst of a people who desperately needed a leader to set an example of godliness in a corrupt world. Zerubbabel, a descendant of King David, had rebuilt the temple. About eighty years later, Ezra returned to Jerusalem from exile with about two thousand Israelites and their families. As you walk with the Lord in His Word today, think about the impact this one man had on a nation.

1. Read Ezra 7–10. List all the actions of Ezra that show his love for God and commitment to what was right and true in the Lord's eyes. (If you need more space, use a journal page in the back of this book.)

2. Ezra continued his ministry with a governor named Nehemiah. Read Nehemiah 8:1–9:3. What is your impression of Ezra? What kind of example did he set for the people? What was the result in the people's lives?

Ezra's example

People's response

3. On days 1 and 2 of this week, you listed everything you learned about the author of Psalm 119. Look at the observations you wrote. In what ways does Ezra's life parallel what you see in the psalm?

4. What impresses you most about Ezra?

5. If you could choose anything from Ezra's life to be true of you, what would you choose?

ADORE GOD IN PRAYER

Ezra knew where to run in times of trouble. What is the prayer of your heart today? Turn to your Prayer Pages and record your prayer. Write the date and choose a verse from your study this week as a promise to claim along with your prayer to the Lord. Take some time today to think about Ezra, and ask God to give you a heart like Ezra that is willing to stand strong in the midst of a godless world.

YIELD YOURSELF TO GOD

God's flowers grow best in places where only an angel would have thought of planting them. Not potbound, tidily, properly trained, is the lily at its fairest. It wants to be where wild rough things crowd it round with ruthless feet. It will not shrink back at fear of their trample. It will touch them lightly, and laugh the while, and at its touch the cactus and aloe show the purpose hidden within them. Ruthless feet are helping hands, lifting the lily up into the light. Perhaps if we could shut our eyes on the world's way of looking at things, and go to sleep with our head on a stone, we should see all the obstructing, all the impossible, changed as it were to a ladder beside us, set on the earth, the top reaching heaven. We need the flower's brave faith and dauntless resolution when we set ourselves to pray.[1]

AMY CARMICHAEL IN *OVERWEIGHTS OF JOY*

It is no accident that you are where you are today. God has a plan. God has a purpose for your life. He desires to do a mighty work in and through you. Draw near to Him in boldness and courage today.

ENJOY HIS PRESENCE

Ezra had an incredible impact in the lives of those around him. How can your life make a difference in your world? Do you have the same sensitivity to sin and reverence before your holy God that Ezra had? As you close your time with the Lord today, write a prayer in your Journal, expressing what is on your heart.

REST IN HIS LOVE

"For the eyes of the LORD move to and fro throughout the earth that He may strongly support those whose heart is completely His" (2 Chronicles 16:9).

let my cry come before you

Let my cry come before You, O LORD;
Give me understanding according to Your Word.
PSALM 119:169

Prepare Your Heart

In every generation there are those rare hearts who will pay the price in time and energy to draw near to their Lord in believing prayer. They are the ones who walk intimately with Him and powerfully influence their world. R. B. Jones says in his book *Rent Heavens*, "God seems to have so ordained that most, if not indeed all, of His activities in the moral and spiritual realms should be the responses of His heart and power to the prayers of His people."[1]

Ezra had a powerful prayer life. Think about the place of prayer in your own life. Do you talk with God at every turn, on every occasion, in all areas of your day and your life? As you begin this time alone with God, meditate on these words from Amy Carmichael in *Toward Jerusalem*:

> O God, renew us in Thy love today,
> For our tomorrow we have not a care,
> Who blessed our yesterday
> Will meet us there.
> But our today is all athirst for Thee,
> Come in the stillness, O Thou heavenly Dew,
> Come Thou to us—to me—
> Revive, renew.[2]

READ AND STUDY GOD'S WORD

Except for four verses, Psalm 119 is a prayer addressed to God. Your need for personal revival will drive you to prayer. And prayer along with God's Word will lead to a revival deep in your heart. Ezra was a man of prayer.

1. The people of Israel had engaged in the sin of intermarriage. God's law banned inter-marriage to prevent His people from being absorbed into the idolatrous cultures that dominated the Middle East at that time. Read Ezra 9:1–10:2. How did Ezra respond to the people's sin?

2. What phrases are significant to you in Ezra's prayer in chapter 9?

3. What do you learn about prayer from Ezra?

4. How can you apply this to your prayer life?

ADORE GOD IN PRAYER

Think about the way Ezra prayed on behalf of the people. He was "praying and making confession, weeping and prostrating himself before the house of God" (Ezra 10:1). He fell on his knees and stretched out his hands to the Lord (see Ezra 9:5). Have you prayed with such an earnestness and humility? Today, in stillness and solitude, draw near to the Lord. Pour out your heart to Him. Ask Him to do something in your life that only He can do. Something mighty. Something that will bring Him great glory. Ask Him today to influence thousands in and through you for the sake of Christ and His gospel.

YIELD YOURSELF TO GOD

Why is the army of the living God still on the battlefield when one charge might give them the victory? Why are His children still wandering hither and thither through a maze, when a solitary word from His lips would bring them into the center of their hopes in heaven? The answer is—they are here that they may *live unto the Lord*, and may bring others to know His love. We remain on earth as sowers to scatter good seed; as ploughmen to break up the fallow ground; as heralds publishing salvation. We are here as the *salt of the earth*, to be a blessing to the world. We are here to glorify Christ in our daily life. We are here as workers for Him, and as *workers together with Him*. Let us see that our life answers its end. Let us live earnest, useful, holy lives, to *the praise of the glory of His grace*.

Meanwhile we long to be with Him, and daily sing:

My heart is with Him on His throne,
And ill can brook delay;
Each moment listening for the voice,
Rise up, and come away.[3]

CHARLES SPURGEON IN *MORNING AND EVENING*

ENJOY HIS PRESENCE

As you close your time with the Lord today, think about the great privilege of walking with Him moment by moment, and the impact that He has in your life and in the lives of those around you. Sing the words of the following hymn to your Lord:

I Need Thee Every Hour

I need thee every hour, most gracious Lord;
no tender voice like thine can peace afford.

Refrain:
I need thee, O I need thee; every hour I need thee;
O bless me now, my Savior, I come to thee.

REST IN HIS LOVE

"Draw near to God and He will draw near to you" (James 4:8).

DEAR FRIEND,

The next two days are your opportunity to review what you have learned this week. You may wish to write your thoughts in your Journal. As you think about the author of Psalm 119, record:

Your most significant insight:

Your favorite quote:

Your favorite verse:

Revival commences with those who in bad times remain good, in godless days remain Christian, in careless years remain constant and who have eternity in their hearts. Revival begins with those who stand firm, like Hezekiah, in an age of godless rejection, in an age when the people do what is right in their own eyes. It begins with the man who stands for that which is true and right and good; but it also requires a man who can see what the state of the church and the nation really is. . . . Revival is always a personal thing, and no one is used in revival who is not himself revived first. That is very important to understand. Those whom God uses in leadership in revival are always men who have met with God in a powerfully personal way and have a burning passion for the glory of God and a life of holiness.[1]

BRIAN H. EDWARDS IN *REVIVAL: A PEOPLE SATURATED WITH GOD*

the cry for revival

week
four

PSALM 119:107

revive me, o Lord

I am exceedingly afflicted;
Revive me, O LORD, according to Your word.
PSALM 119:107

Prepare Your Heart

One of the chief characteristics of revival down through the centuries is a spirit of prayer. Prayer seems to sweep across groups and nations when God pours out His Spirit. In fact, during the Welsh Revival, some said preaching was out of the question because people wanted to pray in the presence of God. When a person or a nation is in trouble, there is only one place to go for real answers and change, and that is to God.

Psalm 119 is a very personal prayer between an individual and God. Sometimes the fire becomes so intense, and the spirit is so low, that almost all hope is gone. The light in the eyes has almost flickered out. It is then that a person will truly turn, heart and soul, to the Lord. Yet it doesn't need to be that way. God is training His servant to turn to Him first, not last. When that servant of God runs to God at every turn in life, then personal spiritual revival characterizes that life. It is life on the highest plane, as Ruth Paxson calls it.[1] It is living a Spirit-filled, extraordinary life in the strength of God. Worries need not drag one to the pit. Circumstances need not plunge a soul into despair. Pleasures need not pull a heart away from God. How is this possible? Only as one walks intimately with the Savior, eyes fixed on Him. That is what God is working in you, even now. He is training you for His highest purposes. Cry out to Him now: *Revive my heart, O Lord!*

As you begin this time with the Lord, turn to Psalm 71, a prayer for personal revival. Think about the words of this psalmist. Then write your own prayer for revival in your Journal.

READ AND STUDY GOD'S WORD

Psalm 119 is a prayer. The psalmist turns to the only one who can answer his need: the Lord. What is the psalmist's prayer? *Revive me, O Lord.* There is much treasure in these words. The key word, *revive*, is repeated sixteen times in this psalm. What does it mean to be revived? That is the subject of your study today.

1. Turn to Psalm 119. The Hebrew word *chayah* is translated *revive* and *live* in most translations. Look at each occurrence of the word *revive* (*live* in the NIV) in this psalm, and record your observations about revival. (The verses are listed below.) Think about how the psalmist desires to be revived and how he has been revived. As you read each verse, circle or underline the word *revive*, or *live*, in your Bible so that it will be easily identifiable when you look at this psalm.

verse 17

verse 25

verse 37

verse 40

verse 50

verse 77

verse 88

verse 93

verse 107

verse 116

verse 144

verse 149

verse 154

verse 156

verse 159

verse 175

2. The word *revive* in the Hebrew means a quickening of heart and soul by God, imparting whatever is necessary to sustain one's spiritual life and restore one to his or her original purpose in life as ordained by God. It includes enjoying life, starting over, rebuilding,
and being refreshed and renewed. Think about what this means for you, the Lord's child.
Write out as many observations as you can from this definition. For example, "This word
means God works in my heart and soul." What else does it mean? Write your insights.

3. Summarize in two to three sentences what you have learned about this psalmist's cry for revival.

4. What is your favorite insight about revival from your study today?

ADORE GOD IN PRAYER

As you look back over the different prayers for revival from the psalmist, which best meets the needs of your heart today? Turn to your Prayer Pages and record that prayer.

YIELD YOURSELF TO GOD

> Now I see that *revival* in its truest sense is an everyday affair right down within the reach of everyday folk to be experienced in our hearts, homes and churches, and in our fields of service. When it does burst forth in greater and more public ways, thank God; but meanwhile we can see to it that we are being ourselves constantly revived persons, which of course also means that others are getting revived in our own circles. By this means God can have channels of revival by the thousands in all the churches of the world. . . . The truth is that revival is really the Reviver in action, and He came two thousands years ago at Pentecost. Revival is not so much a vertical outpouring from heaven, for the Reviver is already here in His temple, the bodies of the redeemed; it is more a horizontal outmoving of the Reviver through these temples into the world.[2]
>
> NORMAN GRUBB IN *CONTINUOUS REVIVAL*

ENJOY HIS PRESENCE

As you walk with the Lord this day, continue to pray: *Revive my heart, O Lord.*

REST IN HIS LOVE

"For God is working in you, giving you the desire to obey him and the power to do what pleases him" (Philippians 2:13, NLT).

according to your Word

My soul cleaves to the dust;
Revive me according to Your word.
PSALM 119:25

Prepare Your Heart

Who is the man or woman God uses in revival? It is the one who knows how to grasp the promises of God and claim them in every circumstance of life. The Word of God is written for you. Its promises belong to you. The Lord loves it when people claim His promises. He loves you to be bold in your activity with His Word.

When the psalmist prays to be revived "according to Your word," he is claiming God's promise to revive. He is saying that God has promised to revive him, so now he is asking for what God has promised. Revival is not the psalmist's idea; it is God's idea first. In claiming God's promise to revive, the psalmist has made His promise the greatest thing in his circumstance and is standing on it by faith. The promise has become a firm foundation, a rock, where nothing can move him.

Charles Spurgeon was called the "Prince of Preachers." He preached at least 3,500 sermons, and it was said that he never repeated himself. His text was always the Word of God. He loved the Bible. He said this about the Word: "There are hundreds of texts in the Bible which remain like virgin summits, whereon the foot of the preacher has never stood. I might also say that the major part of the Word of God is in that condition: it is still an Eldorado unexplored, a land whose dust is gold. After thirty-five years I find that the quarry of Holy Scripture is inexhaustible, I seem hardly to have begun to labor in it!"[1]

Do you love God's Word? Do you have the habit of underlining certain verses that you are holding as your own? Have you ever taken the opportunity to write a date or a name next to certain promises to claim them for a life situation? Today, in your quiet time with the Lord, ask Him to make His Word come alive to you. In every circumstance, always take God's promise in His Word and calculate it as greater than anything you face in life.

READ AND STUDY GOD'S WORD

Our subject is personal spiritual revival. The one who is revived is one who knows how to hold on to God's promises. God and His Word are the center of attention. Today you will look at what it means to claim God's promises in your own life.

1. It is exciting when you come in contact with someone who is bold with the promises of God. One of the greatest characteristics of those men and women of God whose lives are recorded in God's Word is that they knew what God said and they held on to it no matter what. Abraham was bold with God's promises, and God made some big promises to him. In fact, God even repeated His promises to Abraham. In Abraham's situation, those promises seemed impossible. Look at the following passages. Record what God promised Abraham and why the promise seemed impossible to him.

Scripture	The Promise to Abraham	Why It Seemed Impossible
Genesis 11:29–12:3		
Genesis 15		
Genesis 17:1-8		
Genesis 18:10-15		

2. God's promise has its full power when tested. You never know its richness until you are in a circumstance that forces you to make a choice. Which is more true: God's promise, or your feelings and circumstances? In Abraham's case, his faith in God's promise was tested. Turn to Genesis 22:1-19. As you read about this event in Abraham's life, underline phrases in your Bible where Abraham was holding on to God's promises. Where do you see his faith demonstrated?

3. What can you know about God's promise to you? Look at the following verses and write down what you learn.

1 Kings 8:56

Nehemiah 9:6-8

2 Corinthians 1:20

2 Corinthians 7:1

2 Peter 1:4

4. *Optional:* How can you know that something in God's Word is a promise for you? A promise is God giving His Word about Himself, His ways, and His character. Look at the following verses as examples of God's promises to you. If you are short on time today, choose one of the verses as an example of God's promise.

Acts 2:37-39

Philippians 4:6-7

Philippians 4:13

Philippians 4:19

2 Peter 3:13

1 John 2:25

ADORE GOD IN PRAYER

When you pray, do you take God at His Word and claim His promises? Talk with the Lord today about His promises as they relate to your situation. Thank Him for the truthfulness and trustworthiness of His Word. Claim those promises as given specifically to you today, right where you are. You might turn to your Prayer Pages and look at the requests you have written. There is a place to record a passage of Scripture. Write a promise of Scripture next to those prayer requests as the Lord leads. Then pray: *Revive me according to Your word.*

YIELD YOURSELF TO GOD

In his devotional *Faith's Checkbook*, Charles Spurgeon said,

> A promise from God may very instructively be compared to a check payable to order. It is given to the believer with the view of bestowing upon him some good thing. It is not meant that he should read it over comfortably, and then be finished with it. *No, he is to treat the promise as a reality, as a man treats a check.* He is to take the promise, and endorse it with his own name by personally receiving it as true. He is by faith to accept it as his own. He sets to his seal that God is true, and true as to this particular word of promise. He goes further, and believes that he has the blessing in having the sure promise of it and therefore he puts his name to it to testify to the receipt of the blessing. This done, he must believingly present the promise to the Lord, as a man presents a check at the counter of the Bank. He must plead it by prayer, expecting to have it fulfilled. If he has come to Heaven's bank at the right date, he will receive the promised amount at once. If the date should happen to be further on, he must patiently wait till its arrival; but meanwhile he may count the promise as money, for the Bank is sure to pay when the due time arrives. Some fail to place the endorsement of faith upon the check, and so they get nothing; and others are slack in presenting it, and these also receive nothing. This is not the fault of the promise, but of those who do not act with it in a commonsense, businesslike manner. *God has given no pledge which He will not redeem, and encouraged no hope which He will not fulfill.*

This word, we must not only receive, but keep; not only have, but hold (Jn. 8:51). We must keep it in mind and memory, keep it in love and affection, keep in it as our way, keep to it as our rule.[2]

MATTHEW HENRY IN *MATTHEW HENRY'S COMMENTARY OF THE WHOLE BIBLE*

ENJOY HIS PRESENCE

You have been thinking about grasping God's promises for your own today. This expression of faith, claiming the promises of God, will be one of God's great tools in your life to revive your heart. Think about the words of the following hymn as you close your time with the Lord. If you know the music, sing this hymn to the Lord as a strong affirmation of your faith in Him. Declare your love and praise and worship of your King to Him today. God bless you as you rejoice in this day that the Lord has made.

Standing on the Promises

Standing on the promises of Christ my King,
through eternal ages let his praises ring;
glory in the highest, I will shout and sing,
standing on the promises of God.

Refrain:
Standing, standing, standing on the promises of Christ my Savior;
standing, standing, I'm standing on the promises of God.

Standing on the promises that cannot fail,
when the howling storms of doubt and fear assail,
by the living Word of God I shall prevail,
standing on the promises of God.

Refrain

REST IN HIS LOVE

"For by these He has granted to us His precious and magnificent promises, so that by them you may become partakers of the divine nature, having escaped the corruption that is in the world by lust" (2 Peter 1:4).

in Your ways

Turn away my eyes from looking at vanity,
And revive me in Your ways.
PSALM 119:37

Prepare Your Heart

A. W. Tozer was one of those rare men who wanted nothing more in life than to know God. Knowing God was his passion and prize. At the age of fifteen, while walking home from his job, he heard a street preacher say, "If you don't know how to be saved . . . just call on God." That was all Tozer needed to hear. He immediately went home, climbed the stairs to the attic, and gave his life to the Lord.

At twenty-one, Tozer married. With no formal education, he began pastoring a small storefront church. His preaching was powerful. With determination fueled by the Holy Spirit, he educated himself with years of diligent study and continual seeking of God. His forty-four-year ministry included editing *Alliance Weekly*, writing numerous books, and pastoring Chicago's Southside Alliance Church. His heart beat for God. He was known as a man of prayer. He could often be seen during the week walking the aisles of the sanctuary or facedown on the floor praying. Some said he spent more time on his knees than at his desk.

Tozer died in 1963 at the age of sixty-six. Beneath his name on his gravestone are the words, "A Man of God." What more wonderful claim to fame can any person have than to be called a man or woman of God? It is the greatest achievement of all—much more than acquiring billions of dollars or owning the largest company in the world. It is the man or woman of God who will one day hear the words, "Well done, good and faithful servant"[1] when he or she stands face to face with the King of kings and Lord of lords.

What makes men and women of God? They know their God. As a result, they are able to put their trust in Him. The true cry for revival not only claims the promise of God; it also cries out to know the character and ways and Person of God. Intimacy with God. That is His grand design—that you would know Him.

As you have already learned, personal spiritual revival restores people to their true purpose as ordained by God. The one who cries for revival comes to the place where he or she cries out to know His ways. Intimacy with God brings spiritual growth. Spiritual growth ultimately results in becoming the man or woman that God wants you to be.

Do you cry out to know the Lord and His ways? Is that your heart's desire? Take time today to think about your desire to know God. Do you see the greatness of being called a man or woman of God? Will you make Him your passion and prize?

READ AND STUDY GOD'S WORD

What a great purpose God has given us: to know Him. It is a grand, unending adventure until we see Him face to face. We know Him, only to desire Him even more.

1. Moses had such a thirst for God that he would not let Him go until he could see God. God was pleased with that request. Turn to Exodus 33:11-23. Imagine what this must have been like for Moses. Record his prayer and God's response.

Moses' Prayer	God's Response

2. Look at the following verses and record what you learn about this one great thing in life: to know God.

Psalm 46:10

Jeremiah 9:23-24

John 17:3

3. The psalmist in Psalm 119:37 wants his eyes to turn away from vain things so that he might know the Lord. What things might be considered "vain things" that take one's eyes off God and the pursuit of God? Is there anything in your life that is hindering or distracting you from pursuing God?

4. Are you willing today to take your eyes off that distraction in order to pursue God more passionately? You may wish to write a prayer in your Journal in response to God and His Word in your life today.

ADORE GOD IN PRAYER

Today is the day to be still and know that He is God (see Psalm 46:10). Sit or walk with the Lord in silence. Then begin to worship Him, naming what you know about His character and ways. Remember with Him all that He has done in your life. Pray the words of the psalmist: *Revive me in Your ways.*

YIELD YOURSELF TO GOD

> God is a person, and in the deep of His mighty nature He thinks, wills, enjoys, feels, loves, desires and suffers as any other person may. In making Himself known to us He stays by the familiar pattern of personality. He communicates with us through the avenues of our minds, our wills and our emotions. The continuous and unembarrassed interchange of love and thought between God and the soul of the redeemed man is the throbbing heart of New Testament religion.[2]
>
> A. W. TOZER IN *THE PURSUIT OF GOD*

As we all know, the condition of a country depends upon the character of its rulers. The state of an army depends upon the officers who command it. And the more absolute the government, the more this is the case. We can see how it must be, therefore, that everything in the universe depends upon the sort of Creator and Ruler who has brought that universe into existence. The whole welfare of human beings is bound up with the character of their Creator. If the God who created us is a good God, then everything must be all right for us. After all, a good God cannot ordain anything but good. But if He is a bad God, a careless God, or an unkind God, then we cannot be sure that anything is right. We can have no peace or comfort anywhere. The true ground for peace and comfort is only to be found in the sort of God we have. Therefore, we need first of all to find out what is His name, or in other words, what is His character—in short, what sort of God He is.

HANNAH WHITALL SMITH IN THE GOD OF ALL COMFORT

How well do you know your God? Will you engage in the hands-on pursuit of knowing your Lord?

ENJOY HIS PRESENCE

Close your time with the Lord by meditating on the words of Moses: "Let me know Your ways that I may know You, so that I may find favor in Your sight" (Exodus 33:13). Knowing God is an integral element in your cry for revival. Think about this one great desire in life as you go about your day. When it comes to your mind, turn your thoughts to the Lord and talk to Him.

REST IN HIS LOVE

"One thing I have asked from the LORD, that I shall seek: that I may dwell in the house of the LORD all the days of my life, to behold the beauty of the LORD and to meditate in His temple" (Psalm 27:4).

through Your righteousness

Behold, I long for Your precepts; revive me through Your righteousness.
PSALM 119:40

Prepare Your Heart

The psalmist of Psalm 119 cries out to God for personal revival. He has claimed the promise for it. He has asked to know God—the high calling in life. Now he cries for God's righteousness. Why? Because of sin. The only answer for sin is God's righteousness.

It's not good enough to be made better than we once were. As good as we can get on our own is a long distance from the holiness and righteousness of God. He is perfect, majestic, holy, and just. The light of His splendor is blinding to natural man. People, on their own, cannot stand before God. Yet God has set eternity in our hearts. We are made in God's image and are meant to belong to Him, but our sin separates us from Him. So what can we do? Nothing. Only God can make it right. The perfection, holiness, and righteousness from God that is to be ours can come only from outside ourselves. We can have God's splendor only after the penalty for our sin is paid. We must be redeemed from our hopeless state. We are imprisoned by sin and its penalty of death as we stand before a just and holy God. Declared guilty. No hope of release. Except for one thing.

One powerful Person has changed everything for us: Jesus Christ, our Rescuer and Redeemer. He did what it took to free us from the grip of sin and death. He came to earth, was nailed to a cross, and died as others watched. He was the unblemished Lamb who took all our sins upon Himself and died the death that those sins deserved. Because He died for every one of our sins, He can now give us what we need to live forever with Him: the righteousness of God. That is why He is called Savior. He saved us.

Do you understand why He is what life is all about? The whole Bible, Old and New Testaments, centers on one Person: Jesus Christ. The Old Testament points to His coming, and the New Testament explains His life and points to His return, when He will usher in the new heaven and earth, and we will live with Him forever. How many people skip merrily through life and miss the whole point? It's like watching thousands head toward a cliff, oblivious of both the danger and the bridge that could cross it.

The righteousness of God is the answer for your sin today. Meditate on the words of this great hymn in preparation for your time with God:

Hallelujah, What a Savior!

Man of Sorrows! what a name
for the Son of God, who came
ruined sinners to reclaim.
Hallelujah! What a Savior!

Bearing shame and scoffing rude,
in my place condemned he stood;
sealed my pardon with his blood.
Hallelujah! What a Savior!

Guilty, vile, and helpless we;
spotless Lamb of God was he;
full atonement can it be?
Hallelujah! What a Savior!

Lifted up was he to die;
"It is finished!" was his cry;
now in heaven exalted high.
Hallelujah! What a Savior!

When he comes, our glorious King,
all his ransomed home to bring,
then anew this song we'll sing:
Hallelujah! What a Savior!

PHILIP BLISS

READ AND STUDY GOD'S WORD

Today you are going to have the opportunity to meditate on some verses about God's righteousness and holiness. It is a time to think about the beauty and radiance and majesty of your God. If you were to have a window into heaven today, what would you see? The glimpses of heaven that God has given us in His Word are filled primarily with worship. The presence of

God inspires worship. His holiness is beyond comprehension.

1. When God called Isaiah to a great task, He gave him an awesome vision of Himself. Turn to Isaiah 6:1-9. What did Isaiah see, what was his response, and what did God do when He saw Isaiah's response?

What Isaiah saw

Isaiah's response

What God did

What is the righteousness of God? The Hebrew word *tsdaqah* refers to God's standard, which expresses His holy, just, loving, gracious nature. You might think of His standard as His expectation that comes from who He is. It is perfection. He is the Lawgiver and abides by His own standards.[1] Everything God does is right. It's difficult for fallen humans to understand perfection in someone. Only God is perfect. He sets the standard. He is the uncreated Creator of the universe, so His standard is the only true standard. Things that run contrary to His standard are mere opinion and will fall when held up against God's standard.

The New Testament word for righteousness is *dikaiosune*. It means the state of being right before God. When God makes believers righteous by uniting them with Christ, He qualifies them to share in His own life: His love, grace, mercy, peace, joy, holiness, and righteousness. The New Testament writers view righteousness in a legal sense, especially in the book of Romans. Because of what Jesus did on the cross, when we receive Him into our life, we are declared righteous. This declaration is possible because we are now placed in Christ, united with Him in His death and resurrection, and raised in Him to new life. Thus God requires righteousness and also provides righteousness through Jesus Christ.

2. Record what you learn about God's righteousness from the following verses. How can you be righteous ("made right with God," NLT), and what happens as a result?

Romans 1:16-17

Romans 3:21-28

Romans 10:8-11

2 Corinthians 5:21

Philippians 3:8-9

2 Peter 3:13

Optional verses for a study on righteousness: You may use your Journal Pages to record your insights related to righteousness as seen in the following verses: Matthew 6:33; Acts 17:30-31; Acts 24:24-25; Romans 4:3-8; 1 Corinthians 1:30; 2 Timothy 4:7-8; 1 Peter 2:24-25; 3:14-17; 1 John 3:7-8.

3. What did you learn about righteousness today that was most significant to you?

4. Why do you think the cry for revival includes a cry for God's righteousness? In what way does God's righteousness bring about personal revival?

ADORE GOD IN PRAYER

Pray today about your own sin and the folly of it. Oh that we would long for God's way and put away the temporal pleasures of this world. Let us together ask God to lift our eyes above these things to the things of God's kingdom and to give us His desires and ways. Pray today: *Revive me through Your righteousness.*

YIELD YOURSELF TO GOD

If God announces the gift of righteousness apart from works, why do you keep mourning over your bad works, your failures? Do you not see that it is because you still have hopes in these works of yours that you are depressed and discouraged by their failure? If you truly saw and believed that God is reckoning righteous the *ungodly* who believe on Him, you would fairly hate your struggles to be *better;* for you would see that your dreams of good works have not at all commended you to God, and that your bad works do not at all hinder you from believing on Him, that justifies the ungodly!

Therefore, on seeing your failures, you should say, I am nothing but a failure; but God is dealing with me on another principle altogether than my works, good or bad,— a principle not involving my works, but based only on the work of Christ for me. I am anxious, indeed, to be pleasing to God and to be filled with His Holy Spirit; but I am not at all justified, or accounted righteous, by these things. God, in justifying me, acted wholly and only on Christ's blood-shedding on my behalf.

Therefore, I have this double attitude: first, I know that Christ is in Heaven before God for me, and that I stand in the value before God of His finished work; that God sees me nowhere else but in this dead, buried, and risen Christ, and that His favor is toward me in Christ, and is limitless and eternal.

Then, second, toward the work of the Holy Spirit in me, my attitude is, a desire to be guided into the truth, to be obedient thereto, and to be chastened by God my Father if disobedient; to learn to pray in the Spirit, to walk by the Spirit, and to be filled with a love for the Scriptures and for the saints and for all men.

Yet none of these things justifies me! I had justification from God as a sinner, not as a saint! My saintliness does not increase it, nor, praise God, do my failures decrease it!

WILLIAM NEWELL IN *ROMANS, VERSE BY VERSE*

ENJOY HIS PRESENCE

What is your response as you see God's righteousness? Think about how Isaiah responded to His awesome God. Include in your cry for revival today the prayer, *Revive me through Your righteousness.*

REST IN HIS LOVE

"I delight greatly in the LORD; my soul rejoices in my God. For he has clothed me with garments of salvation and arrayed me in a robe of righteousness" (Isaiah 61:10, NIV).

according to Your lovingkindness

Consider how I love Your precepts;
Revive me, O Lord, according to Your lovingkindness.
Psalm 119:159

Prepare Your Heart

What do you do if you find yourself in an impossible situation with seemingly no one to help? Darlene Diebler Rose and her husband, missionaries in New Guinea, were taken captive by the Japanese during World War II. Darlene's husband was taken first, and she never saw him again. Darlene went to a prison camp, where she endured intense suffering. She received meager food rations, sometimes a mere handful of rice in a day.

One day she looked out her window and watched some of the other prisoners walking in the yard. One in particular caught her eye. She saw the prisoner walk by a bush. As the prisoner walked by, a hand came from the bush with a banana. The prisoner grabbed it and hid it under her clothing. Because of Darlene's hunger, she could not get that banana out of her mind. She thought, "Lord, if I could just have one banana." She reasoned that it was virtually impossible to get a banana. But she continued to pray that somehow the Lord would bring her a banana. Some days later, she heard footsteps walking down the hall toward her cell. The door opened and she heard something thrown onto the floor of her cell. What do you think it was? Bananas! A huge clump of bananas! Ninety-two of them. That is just one of the many ways the Lord met this young woman with His love.[1]

In the depth of suffering, the cry for revival includes a cry for the Lord's lovingkindness. You need His lovingkindness every day of your life. This is His *hesed*, or covenant love. It never fails and is forever compassionate. This love gave everything to gain your salvation. And this merciful and compassionate love will revive you when you suffer. God comforts you in pain, strengthens you in weakness, gives you peace in stress, and allows you rest when you cannot go on. Do you need God's lovingkindness? Ask Him now to revive you in His lovingkindness.

117

READ AND STUDY GOD'S WORD

Nothing in this world compares with God's love for you. Nothing will so revive you in the midst of trials as the experience of His great love. The best way to understand God's love is in Jesus Christ. Today you will look at the love of God in Christ.

1. When Jesus walked this earth, He showed His love in tangible ways as He came in contact with different people. Record what you see in the following passages about the people's suffering, how they needed the Lord, how Jesus demonstrated His love, and the result.

Scripture Passage	Need of Individual(s)	Demonstration of Love	Result
Matthew 9:1-8			
Matthew 18:12-14			
Matthew 20:29-34			
John 11:1-46			
John 20:1-18			

2. In what ways does the Lord tangibly express His love to you in the midst of your trials? Look at the following verses and record what God does in the power of the Holy Spirit, from His heart of love for you.

Isaiah 40:11

Ezekiel 34:16

John 15:11

John 16:33

2 Corinthians 1:3-5

Philippians 4:13

3. In what ways has God revived you with His love?

ADORE GOD IN PRAYER

Think about those in your life who need the Lord's lovingkindness. Write their names on one of your Prayer Pages. Bring each one to the Lord and ask Him to revive them in His lovingkindness.

YIELD YOURSELF TO GOD

Through a sequence of human events (divinely inspired), the God and Father of our Lord Jesus Christ leads us into a state of interior devastation. When we are like this, it is highly probable (though not inevitable) that we become more prayerful. Up to now we had not been praying in depth; now we are truly praying. We might not be saying all that many prayers, and we might not be following the set formulas that we presumed were prayer, but we are praying as never before. God is drawing us closer to Himself.[2]

BRENNAN MANNING IN *THE SIGNATURE OF JESUS*

Do not tell me that God the Father does not love you as well as he does Christ: the point can be settled by the grandest matter of fact that ever was. When there was a choice between Christ and his people which should die of the two, the Father freely delivered up his own Son that we might live through him. Oh, what a meeting there must have been of the seas of love that day, when God's great love to us came rolling in like a glorious springtide, and his love to his Son came rolling in at the same time. If they had met and come into collision, we cannot imagine the result; but when they both took to rolling together in one mighty torrent, what a stream of love was there! The Lord Jesus sank that we might swim, he sank that we might rise; and now we are borne onward for ever by the mighty sweep of infinite love into an everlasting blessedness which tongues and lips can never fully set forth. Oh, be ravished with this. Be carried away with it; be in ecstasy at love so amazing, so divine: the Father loves you even as he loves his Son; after the same manner and sort he loveth all his redeemed.[3]

CHARLES SPURGEON IN HIS SERMON "LOVE AND I—A MYSTERY"

What revival in the heart there is with God's love. Romans 5:8 says, "God demonstrates His own love toward us, in that while we were yet sinners, Christ died for us." That same love that saves you surely will minister to you in the fiery trial.

Blessed be the God and Father of our Lord Jesus Christ, the Father of mercies and God of all comfort, who comforts us in all our affliction so that we will be able to comfort those who are in any affliction with the comfort with which we ourselves are comforted by God. For just as the sufferings of Christ are ours in abundance, so also our comfort is abundant through Christ. (2 Corinthians 1:3-5)

ENJOY HIS PRESENCE

How do you need the Lord's lovingkindness today? Write a prayer to Him in your Journal, expressing all that is on your heart.

REST IN HIS LOVE

"I have loved you with an everlasting love; therefore I have drawn you with lovingkindness" (Jeremiah 31:3).

DEAR FRIEND,

This week you looked at the psalmist's cry for revival. Look back over your week of study and summarize what the psalmist was asking from God when he ran to Him for revival.

What were your most meaningful discoveries this week as you spent time with the Lord? Most meaningful insight:

Most meaningful devotional reading:

Most meaningful verse:

More life is the cure for all our ailments. Only the Lord can give it. He can bestow it, bestow it at once, and do it according to his word, without departing from the usual course of this grace, as we see it mapped out in the Scriptures. . . . When a person is depressed in spirit, weak, and bent towards the ground, the main thing is to increase his stamina and put more life into him; then his spirit revives, and his whole body becomes erect. In reviving the life, the whole man is renewed. Shaking off the dust is a little thing by itself, but when it follows upon quickening, it is a blessing of the greatest value; just as good spirits which flow from established health are among the choicest of our mercies. . . . The word of God shows us that he who first made us must keep us alive, and it tells us of the Spirit of God who through the ordinances pours fresh life into our souls.[1]

CHARLES SPURGEON IN *THE TREASURY OF DAVID*, VOL. 3

the path to revival

week
five

PSALM 119:50

your Word has revived me

This is my comfort in my affliction,
That Your word has revived me.
PSALM 119:50

Prepare Your Heart

How does God answer in the dark of the night when He hears the cry of His child? How does He reach through the heavens and touch the heart of the afflicted? What can change the face of discouragement? What can revive the heart? One thing: the Word of God. When you are in what can only be called the dark night of the soul, God's Word can make its way to the place of pain and, like a healing balm, soothe and comfort like nothing else can. The Word of God is a treasure greater than all the riches in the world.

Where do you run in the time of trouble? The greatest thing you can learn is to run to God in His Word. In the Word you will find the Lord. In the Word He will speak to you. Do you long to hear His voice? Open the pages of the Bible, and listen for His comfort, His encouragement, His wisdom, and His guidance. He will meet you there.

As you begin this time with Him, turn to Psalm 19. Meditate on what it says about God's Word. What is your favorite verse in this psalm? Write it out, word for word. Thank the Lord for His Word today.

READ AND STUDY GOD'S WORD

Psalm 119 displays the magnificence of God's Word. Nowhere in the Bible is so much said in one place about the Word of God. If the Word of God is the highlight and this is a psalm asking for revival, then there is a connection between the two. The psalmist says he is revived by God in His Word: "This is my comfort in my affliction, that Your word has revived me" (verse 50); "I will never forget Your precepts, for by them You have revived me" (verse 93). God promises to revive His children, and He does it with His Word.

This week you will see the magnificence of God's Word. Hold these truths close to your heart. There is no greater occupation for the child of God than to be a student of His Word. When life comes down to a choice between time in God's Word or earthly pleasures at the expense of that time, you need to choose to open the Bible and meet God there. You will reap eternal benefit and your life will display the result. This time will determine whether or not you become the man or woman that God wants you to be. Knowing God in His Word is more challenging and rewarding than climbing the highest mountain, achieving the greatest earthly goal, or having all the money in the world. The best decision you will ever make is to know what God says more than you know anything else.

1. Turn to Psalm 119 and look at the following verses. Record the phrases in which the author speaks about what the Word of God has done for him. Mark them in some way in your Bible so you can find them when you return to this psalm in future days.

verse 50

verse 93

2. The psalmist knew the Word of God. Over and over he repeats the phrase, "according to Your word." How could he say "according to Your word" and claim God's promise unless he knew it well? In the verses following, look at what the psalmist claimed or asked for according to God's Word. As you read each of these verses, highlight the phrase "according to Your word" (or "by your Word" and "as you promised," NLT; "according to your promise," NIV). As you make your observations, keep your answers brief, using just a few words to record your insights.

verse 9

verse 25

verse 28

verse 41

verse 58

verse 65

verse 76

verse 91

verse 107

verse 116

verse 149

verse 154

verse 156

verse 169

verse 170

3. How would asking for these things restore a person to the life and purpose of God in the midst of affliction or difficulty?

ADORE GOD IN PRAYER

In what ways do you need revival today? Write what is on your heart using one of the Prayer Pages in the back of this study book. Choose a verse from your study today to claim for your prayer requests. Write that verse in the space provided on your page. As you talk with the Lord today, ask Him to make you a student of His Word. Proclaim to Him that you want to know His Word. Thank Him for the gift of His Word.

YIELD YOURSELF TO GOD

The great tragedy among Christians today is that too many of us are under the Word of God, but not in it for ourselves. I met a man once who had driven his entire family all the way across the country to attend a Bible conference. Amazed, I asked him, "Why did you come so far?" "Because I wanted to get under the Word of God," he said. On the face of it, that sounds wonderful. But later it hit me: Here was a man willing to drive twelve hundred miles to get under the Word of God; but was he just as willing to walk across his living room floor, pick up a Bible, and get into it for himself? You see, there's no question that believers need to sit under the teaching of God's Word. But that ought to be a stimulus — not a substitute — for getting into it ourselves.[1]

HOWARD HENDRICKS AND WILLIAM HENDRICKS IN *LIVING BY THE BOOK*

Teaching others how to study the Bible for themselves is like leading a tour through mountain grandeur. Every feature is virtually indescribable. One can only feel the greatness. Though we climb the hills and breathe the air, we struggle for words to describe the adventure. Yet whereas the awesome magnitude of the biblical terrain belittles our security blanket of pride, its attraction never pales. Exposure to that powerful message never ceases to stir our spirit. . . . The study of the Bible is de rigueur for the Christian. More than a duty, it provides protection for the daily battle, comfort for dashed hopes, and continuing education for a life that is worth living.[2]

HOWARD HENDRICKS IN THE PREFACE OF *LIVING BY THE BOOK*

One of the greatest needs in the church today is to come back to the Scriptures as the basis of authority, and to study them prayerfully in dependence on the Holy Spirit. When we read God's Word, we fill our hearts with His words, and God is speaking to us.[3]

BILLY GRAHAM IN *WHAT THE BIBLE IS ALL ABOUT* BY HENRIETTA C. MEARS

Where do you run in a time of trouble? Has there ever been a time when you have run to the Lord in His Word and He has spoken to you through a passage of Scripture?

ENJOY HIS PRESENCE

How well do you know God's Word? What promises could you claim "according to His word" today in relation to your own circumstances? Will you determine in your heart to be like those at the church of Berea who "were more noble-minded than those in Thessalonica, for they received the word with great eagerness, examining the Scriptures daily to see whether these things were so" (Acts 17:11)?

REST IN HIS LOVE

"For it is not an idle word for you; indeed it is your life. And by this word you will prolong your days in the land, which you are about to cross the Jordan to possess" (Deuteronomy 32:47).

o how i love Your law!

O how I love Your law!
It is my meditation all the day.
PSALM 119:97

Prepare Your Heart

Dr. J. Edwin Orr told a story about a young shoe salesman who went to the superintend-ent of the Plymouth Congregational Church in the mid-1800s and asked if he could teach Sunday school. The superintendent said he was sorry, but he had too many Sunday school teachers. The young man protested that he wanted to get started right away. The superintendent said that if he really wanted to teach, he could start a class by gathering together a group, taking them out to the country, and if they could stay together, he could then bring them to the church.

The young shoe salesman gathered a group together, took them to a beach at Lake Michigan, taught them Bible verses and Bible games, then took them to the Congregational church. His name was Dwight Lyman Moody. That was the beginning of a ministry that lasted forty years. God used D. L. Moody to bring the gospel of Jesus Christ to more than one hundred million people during his lifetime. He spoke to at least 1.5 million people dur-ing a four-month period in London in 1875. He was the first mass evangelist and pioneered the way for Bible conferences in America with his popular Northfield conferences. He began the Chicago Bible Institute, which was renamed Moody Bible Institute upon his death. One of the great secrets to his zeal for the Lord and the vast scope of his ministry was his intense love for God's Word. During the Great Chicago Fire on October 8, 1871, he was interested in saving only one item—his Bible.[1]

In his article "How to Study the Bible," Moody said, "I never saw a useful Christian who was not a student of the Bible. If a man neglects his Bible, he may pray and ask God to use him in His work, but God cannot make much use of him; for there is not much for the Holy Spirit to work upon. We must have the Word itself, which is sharper than any two-edged sword."[2]

How is your love for the Word of God? Is it intense and passionate? Do you love to open the pages of your Bible and spend much time listening to what God has to say to you? As you begin your time with the Lord today, ask Him to fan the flame of desire in your heart to draw near to Him in His Word.

READ AND STUDY GOD'S WORD

The psalmist of Psalm 119 writes of his intense passion for God's Word in almost every verse. He clings to it; he holds it fast and waits for it. Today your goal is to see his love for the Word.

1. Look at the following verses in Psalm 119 and record what the author says about his desire for the Word and what he does with the Word. As you read each verse, underline the significant phrases in your Bible about his desire (for example, "I shall delight in Your commandments, which I love," verse 47, emphasis added). Doing this will help those phrases stand out to you as you review the psalm and will help the words sink into your heart. It will also help slow you down to observe God's truth and hear Him speak.

verse 11

verse 16

verse 20

verse 24

verse 31

verse 42

verse 47

verse 48

verse 49

verse 81

verse 93

verse 97

verse 103

verse 111

verse 119

verse 143

verse 161

verse 162

verse 167

2. Summarize what you see in the psalmist's feelings about the Word.

3. How do you think he developed such a love for the Word of God?

4. How do you think a love for the Word will make a difference in your relationship with the Lord?

ADORE GOD IN PRAYER

My Father,
In a world of created changeable things,
Christ and his Word alone remain unshaken.
O to forsake all creatures,
to rest as a stone on him the foundation,
to abide in him, be borne up by him!
For all my mercies come through Christ,
who has designed, purchased, promised, effected them.
How sweet it is to be near him, the Lamb,
filled with holy affections!
When I sin against thee I cross thy will, love, life,
and have no comforter, no creature, to go to.
My sin is not so much this or that particular evil,
but my continual separation, disunion, distance from thee,
and having a loose spirit towards thee.
But thou hast given me a present, Jesus thy Son,
as mediator between thyself and my soul,
as middle-man who in a pit
holds both him below and him above,
for only he can span the chasm breached by sin,
and satisfy divine justice.
May I always lay hold upon this mediator,
as a realized object of faith,
and alone worthy by his love to bridge the gulf.
Let me know that he is dear to me by his Word;
I am one with him by the Word on his part,
and by faith on mine;
If I oppose the Word I oppose my Lord when he is most near;
If I receive the Word I receive my Lord wherein he is nigh.
O thou who hast the hearts of all men in thine hand,
form my heart according to the Word,
according to the image of thy Son,
So shall Christ the Word, and his Word, be my strength and comfort.[3]

FROM *THE VALLEY OF VISION*

YIELD YOURSELF TO GOD

I can imagine some persons asking, "How can I get to be in love with the Bible?" Well,
if you will only rouse yourselves to the study of it, and ask God's assistance, He will

assuredly help you. . . . Read the Bible as if you were seeking for something of value. It is a good deal better to take a single chapter and spend a month on it, than to read the Bible at random for a month. . . . I have carried my Bible with me a good many years. It is worth more to me than all the Bibles in this place, and I will tell you why; because I have got so many passages marked in it, and if I am called upon to speak at anytime, I am ready. I have got these little words in the margin, and they are a sermon to me. Whether I speak about faith, hope, charity, assurance, or any subject whatever, it all comes back to me. Every child of God ought to be like a soldier, and always hold himself in readiness; but we can't be ready if we don't study the Bible. So whenever you hear a good thing just put it down, because if it's good for you it will be good for somebody else; and we should pass the coin of heaven round just as we do other current coin.[4]

D. L. MOODY IN "HOW TO STUDY THE BIBLE" IN *THE BIBLE READER'S GUIDE*

Do you live in God's Word? Have you made the Bible your own by underlining certain verses and making notations in the Bible as you study it? Turn to your Journal and write your thoughts about what has challenged you the most in your study today. You might close your Journal writing with a prayer to the Lord, asking Him to give you increased love for His Word.

ENJOY HIS PRESENCE

My Faith Has Found a Resting Place

My faith has found a resting place,
Not in a man-made creed;
I trust the ever living One, That He for me will plead.

Refrain:
I need no other evidence,
I need no other plea;
It is enough that Jesus died
And rose again for me.

Enough for me that Jesus saves,
This ends my fear and doubt;
A sinful soul I come to Him,
He will not cast me out.

Refrain

My soul is resting on the Word,
The living Word of God.
Salvation in my Savior's name,
Salvation through His blood.

Refrain

The great Physician heals the sick,
The lost He came to save;
For me His precious blood He shed,
For me His life He gave.

Refrain

REST IN HIS LOVE

"People need more than bread for their life; real life comes by feeding on every word of the
LORD" (Deuteronomy 8:3, NLT).

above fine gold

Therefore I love Your commandments
Above gold, yes, above fine gold.
PSALM 119:127

Prepare Your Heart

In *The Count of Monte Cristo* by Alexandre Dumas, a young man named Edmond Dantes is unjustly sent to prison. An old man in the prison tells him about a hidden treasure. Edmond escapes, finds the treasure, and becomes the Count of Monte Cristo. The treasure enables the transformation.

Have you ever imagined what it would be like to find buried treasure? Think about how the treasure would change your life. God has given you a treasure that is greater than any found in this world. It is a treasure that will transform you into a man or woman of God. The treasure is God's Word. Today you will look at its magnificence. Its facets take a lifetime to appreciate and enjoy.

The Bible is God's Word. Its sixty-six documents were written over more than sixteen hundred years by more than forty authors. These authors did not write their own words—they wrote God's words. We know that because 2 Timothy 3:16 says, "All Scripture is God-breathed" (NIV) or "inspired" (NASB). Because the Bible is from God, it is *authoritative* (has the right to govern your life and actions), it is *infallible* (dependable, reliable, certain, and trustworthy), and it is *inerrant* (it is true, flawless, and without error). Just think—in a world that is constantly changing, you hold in your hands truth from God that will never change. You can bank your life on it. It is a firm foundation in the midst of the storms of life. God's Word is truer than your feelings and circumstances. If you want to know what God thinks about anything, how He works, and what He desires for you, open the pages of the Bible. It is buried treasure. Buried, because in order to get at it, you must take time to dig deep. The deeper you go, the more you will have. It is there. God is holding it out to you. Now, resolve to go after it.

As you draw near to the Lord today, think about the following words of Charles Spurgeon in *Morning and Evening*. Will you find a quiet resting place and take time with the Word of God? In your Journal, record your response to what he has written.

The person of Jesus is the quiet resting-place of His people, and when we draw near to Him in the breaking of bread, in the hearing of the word, the searching of the Scriptures, prayer, or praise, we find any form of approach to Him to be the return of peace to our spirits. *I hear the words of love, I gaze upon the blood, I see the mighty sacrifice, and I have peace with God. Tis everlasting peace, sure as Jehovah's name, Tis stable as His steadfast throne, forevermore the same; The clouds may go and come, and storms may sweep my sky, This blood-sealed friendship changes not, the cross is ever nigh.*[1]

READ AND STUDY GOD'S WORD

By now you have seen that Psalm 119 is filled with truth about God's Word. You probably noticed the different names for the Word of God. These include *precepts, statutes, commandments, judgments, word, testimonies, law, ways,* and *ordinances.* What is the difference between these words? All are from God and are, therefore, the Word of God. Yet they have distinguishing characteristics. Here are descriptions of each to help you understand Psalm 119 and unfold the beauty of what God has given you in His Word:

- *Precepts:* Commands and ordinances of God having to do with matters of conscience
- *Statutes* (or *principles*, NLT): God's moral law engraved on human hearts. This moral law cannot be changed, and humans are obligated to keep it.
- *Commandments:* This literally means "lodged with us in trust" and is the authoritative word from God.
- *Judgments, ordinances:* The governing aspect of God's Law that judges human thoughts and actions
- *Word:* The declaration of God's mind, revelation of His will, and announcement of His purpose. Herbert Lockyer calls words "the clothing of the thoughts of our mind."[2] This brings out the incredible truth that behind God's Word is God Himself. Therefore, we are never alone when reading the Bible. God is there, speaking by the Holy Spirit, through His Word.
- *Testimonies* (or *decrees*, NLT): The aspect of the law that attests, confirms, and stands as a witness of God's presence among His people
- *Law:* The Torah, which means instruction. Its goal is to direct and guide. It is a rule of conduct that is designed to protect us and cause our lives to flourish.
- *Ways:* God's will and desire that flow from His nature[3]

Read Psalm 119:7-11 and notice how many of these different distinctions of God's Word are used in one passage. It is an amazing thing that God has chosen to reveal Himself to us,

His creation. Rather than being aloof and withdrawn from His creation, He has spoken. He has spoken in three distinct ways to us: through creation, Jesus Christ, and the Word of God.

1. As you begin this time in the Word, think about the amazing fact that God has chosen to speak and reveal Himself to you. Look at the different ways He has spoken, and record your insights in the spaces provided. Describe what you learn about God's revelation and how He has spoken to you.

Creation: Psalm 19:1-6; Romans 1:20

Jesus Christ: Hebrews 1:1-3

The Word of God: 2 Peter 1:20-21

2. What does the psalmist know about God's Word? These are some of the things that keep him coming back, day after day, to hear what God has to say to him. What do you learn about the Word of God from each of the following verses in Psalm 119? Move quickly through these verses, personalize your insights, and keep them brief (for example, "keeps me from sin," verse 11).

verse 11

verse 24

verse 39

verse 45

verse 86

verse 89

verse 96

verse 103

verse 140

verse 144

verse 151

verse 160

verse 162

3. What is your favorite truth about God's Word from this psalm? What does it mean for you in your own life?

4. *Optional:* There are some important things to know about the Bible. These things qualify it to be first on every believer's list of priorities. Look at the following verses and record what you learn.

Deuteronomy 8:3

Matthew 24:35

John 15:7

John 17:17

2 Timothy 3:16-17

Hebrews 4:12

1 Peter 1:23-25

ADORE GOD IN PRAYER

Today, as you talk with the Lord, thank Him for the magnificence of His Word. Ask Him to raise your own view of His Word so that you can learn to trust Him for what He says there.

YIELD YOURSELF TO GOD

It is a grace to know God's commands. They release us from self-made plans and conflicts. They make our steps certain and our way joyful. God gives his commands in order that we may fulfill them, and *his commandments are not burdensome* (I John 5:3) for him who has found all salvation in Jesus Christ. . . . Now we confess our love for the law, we affirm that we gladly keep it, and we ask that we may continue to be kept blameless in it. We do that not in our own power, but we pray it in the name of Jesus Christ who is for us and in us.[4]

DIETRICH BONHOEFFER IN *PSALMS: THE PRAYER BOOK OF THE BIBLE*

ENJOY HIS PRESENCE

Today, as you go through the day, think about the fact that the Lord has spoken to you in creation, Jesus Christ, and His Word. Walk with a spirit of praise and thanksgiving that your God is not distant but personal, and that He has given you the wonderful gift of His Word.

REST IN HIS LOVE

"All Scripture is inspired by God and is useful to teach us what is true and to make us realize what is wrong in our lives. It straightens us out and teaches us to do what is right. It is God's way of preparing us in every way, fully equipped for every good thing God wants us to do" (2 Timothy 3:16-17, NLT).

that i may not sin

Your word I have treasured in my heart,
That I may not sin against You.
PSALM 119:11

Prepare Your Heart

Martin Luther was born in 1483 in Eisleben, Germany. He was training to become a lawyer when he was nearly struck by lightning. This brush with death motivated him to become a monk instead. He joined the Augustinian friars and eventually became a professor of theology at the new university at Wittenberg. He loved theology and the study of God's Word. However, the teachings in the book of Romans frustrated him. At that time, the Church and the pope, not the Bible, held the primary authority in people's lives.

In the quiet of the monastery where he lived, Luther would spend hours studying the book of Romans. One day, God opened up the meaning of this book. He was struck by chapter 1, verse 17: "The just shall live by faith" (KJV). Through that verse, he realized that salvation is a gift received by faith. The verse unveiled to him the mystery of the Christian life.

Luther began preaching the gospel in a small chapel in the square at Wittenberg. There the preaching of the Reformation began. Because of his gift for preaching, the local monasteries sent him as their agent to Rome. Luther was excited, imagining Rome to be a sanctuary of spirituality. But in Rome he discovered the hypocrisy of the Roman priests as they made fun of parishioners in his presence.

The Church had promised a special blessing to all who would ascend on their knees what was called Pilate's Staircase, which had reputedly been miraculously transported from Jerusalem to Rome. While Luther was humbly creeping up the steps on his knees, he heard in his heart the words "the just shall live by faith." Immediately he rose from the steps in shame, realizing that what he was doing had nothing to do with the gospel and that dragging himself up those stairs was a mere superstition. (Sometimes you have to hear a verse of Scripture many times in different contexts for it to have a measurable impact on your life.) In that instant, Luther realized more fully that righteousness came by faith and not by any meritorious act on his part. This insight became the foundation of his theology and the foundation of the Reformation.

Before he understood these words, Luther hated God, feeling that God was punishing him for his sins and torturing Christians with His righteousness. But his eyes were opened when he realized that justification of the sinner came from God's mercy. He saw the Bible with new eyes. He had hated the words "righteousness of God," but now he felt they were the sweetest and most consoling words in the Bible. He said, "Within my heart reigns alone faith in the Lord Jesus Christ who is the beginning, end and middle of all the thoughts that occupy my mind by day and night."[1]

God uses His Word to revive our hearts. Because of Luther's transformed life, our world was blessed with a proper interpretation of how one may be saved: we are justified and saved by grace through faith. When the Word of God makes its impression on our hearts and we adjust our lives to its truth, that dynamic change influences the world.

What impact does God want to make in your heart with His Word? Turn to Isaiah 55:8-11 and meditate on these words from the Lord as a preparation of heart. You may wish to record your insights.

READ AND STUDY GOD'S WORD

God always has a purpose to accomplish with His Word in your life. Even today. As you open the pages of Scripture, the Lord wants to speak to you and change you in the depths of your soul.

1. Turn to Psalm 119 again. Look at what God accomplished in the psalmist's life with His Word. God can and will do the same for you as you draw near to Him. As you record your insights, personalize your answers (for example, "God gives *me* peace with His Word").

verse 9

verse 38

verse 50

verses 98-99

verse 105

verse 130

verse 164

2. In what ways do you think God revived the psalmist with His Word? From looking at these verses, what truths do you think comforted him?

3. Ezekiel was a servant of the Lord who spoke to God's rebellious people when they were exiled to Babylon. One of his visions promised revival. Read Ezekiel 37:1-14. Notice the hope it offers to people who are in a hopeless situation in exile. How did God's Word change everything in the event described here?

4. What do you learn from Ezekiel about what God can do in a hopeless situation?

ADORE GOD IN PRAYER

Today pray the prayer of the psalmist: "Open my eyes, that I may behold wonderful things from Your law" (Psalm 119:18). Think about the truths that comfort you. Thank the Lord for that comfort today.

YIELD YOURSELF TO GOD

As the Word of the Living God it is a living Word, and gives life. It not only calls into existence, but even makes alive again that which is dead. Its quickening power can raise dead bodies, can give eternal life to dead souls. All spiritual life comes through it, for we are born of incorruptible seed by the Word of God that liveth and abideth forever. Here there lies, hidden from many, one of the deepest secrets of the blessing of God's Word — faith in its creative and quickening energy. The Word will work in me the very disposition or grace which it commands or promises. *It worketh effectually in them that believe.* Nothing can resist its power when received into the heart through the Holy Spirit. *It worketh effectually in them that believe.* . . . Everything depends upon the art of receiving that Word into the heart. And in learning this art the first step is: faith in its living, its omnipotence, its creative power. . . . Faith does not look at appearances. By outward appearances it would look most improbable that a Word of God would give life in the soul, would work in us the very grace of which it speaks, would transform our whole character, would fill us with strength. And yet so it is. When once we have learned to believe that the Word can work effectually the very truth it expresses, we have found one of the chief secrets of our Bible study. We shall then receive each word as the pledge and the power of a divine working.[2]

ANDREW MURRAY IN *THE INNER LIFE*

ENJOY HIS PRESENCE
In what ways do you need the reviving power of God's Word in your life today — for comfort, for hope, for peace, for guidance, for insight? Record your thoughts in your Journal.

REST IN HIS LOVE
"For everything that was written in the past was written to teach us, so that through endurance and the encouragement of the Scriptures we might have hope" (Romans 15:4, NIV).

i will meditate on your precepts

I will meditate on Your precepts
And regard Your way.
PSALM 119:15

Prepare Your Heart

Almost every American household contains a Bible. In fact, many have more than one. The Bible is a best-seller. How many of those Bibles are sitting on shelves gathering dust? Statistics show that of those who attend church, only 37 percent ever open their Bibles outside church. How would that statistic change if Bibles were unavailable or even banned?

If you walk down the streets of Oxford today, you will come upon a memorial stone dedicated to William Tyndale. Tyndale lived from 1494 to 1536. He did something that has affected all of us: he translated and published the New Testament in English, sacrificing himself, so that the Word of God could get into the hands of common people.

As a young man, Tyndale was able to read the New Testament because he was a Greek scholar. The words revolutionized his life, and he wanted others to experience what he had. In those days, the Church claimed the sole authority to interpret the Bible for the people. In fact, one man said to young Tyndale that the Bible wasn't even necessary, only the word of the pope. This claim drove Tyndale to accomplish his life work, for it was his desire that even a boy who plowed the ground of England would know more of the Bible than the priests and the pope. He began immediately translating from the original languages a Bible in English.

This did not catch on with the pope, as you might imagine, and Tyndale was forced to flee for his life to Germany. In Germany, he met Martin Luther. At Worms, Germany, Tyndale published his English New Testament in 1526. Copies were smuggled into England in bales of cloth or barrels of merchandise. Even though Church officials gathered many of these New Testaments and burned them, many copies made their way into the hands of the people. They could not stop the spreading of the Word of God. Soon English Bibles were everywhere.

Because of his bold work of translating and publishing the New Testament, Tyndale was forced to hide for fear of his life. One night, while walking outside the home where he was staying in Antwerp, Tyndale was kidnapped and imprisoned in Brussels for sixteen months. On October 6, 1536, he was led to a place of execution, tied to a stake, strangled to death, and burned. His last words were, "Oh Lord, open the king of England's eyes."

What an awesome thing it is to have the privilege to read and study God's Word. So many have given their lives that you might hold the precious Word of God in your hands and study it for yourself. Today, as you draw near to the Lord in your quiet time, ask Him to quiet your heart that you might hear Him speak in His Word. Thank Him for the wonderful gift of the Bible.

READ AND STUDY GOD'S WORD

Paul challenged Timothy to "be diligent to present yourself approved to God as a workman who does not need to be ashamed, accurately handling the word of truth" (2 Timothy 2:15). He said in Colossians 3:16 to "let the word of Christ richly dwell within you." That word *richly* means *extravagantly*. We should be extravagant with the Word of God. How can you be a worker of the Word, handling it accurately and extravagantly living in it? The author of Psalm 119 offers ideas.

1. Turn to this wonderful psalm again today. You have spent much time going from verse to verse, looking at different truths about the Word. You have been reading with specific goals in mind, like a detective looking for clues. Today you will see how the psalmist lived in God's Word. How did he know it so well? Look at the following verses in Psalm 119 and record what the author did with the Word.

verse 11

verse 16

verse 31

verses 48, 97, 148

verse 94

verse 112

verse 162

verses 166-168

verse 172

2. What do you think it means to meditate on the Word of God? The word *meditate* is *siach* in Hebrew and means to ponder, muse, declare, speak, talk, or go over a matter in one's mind.[1] In practical terms, how does one do this with God's Word?

3. What is one idea from the psalmist that you might try in your quiet time to make the Word of God a more dominant feature of your life?

Adore God in Prayer
Use the words of the psalmist to form your prayer today. Ask God to revolutionize your heart and life with His Word by the power of His Holy Spirit.

> Teach me, O LORD, the way of Your statutes,
> And I shall observe it to the end.
> Give me understanding, that I may observe Your law
> And keep it with all my heart.
> Make me walk in the path of Your commandments,
> For I delight in it.
> Incline my heart to Your testimonies
> And not to dishonest gain.
> Turn away my eyes from looking at vanity,
> And revive me in Your ways.
> Establish Your word to Your servant,
> As that which produces reverence for You. (Psalm 119:33-38)

Yield Yourself to God

Devotional study is not so much a technique as a spirit. It is the spirit of eagerness which seeks the mind of God; it is the spirit of humility which listens readily to the voice of God; it is the spirit of adventure which pursues earnestly the will of God; it is the spirit of adoration which rests in the presence of God.[2]

MERRILL C. TENNEY IN GALATIANS: THE CHARTER OF CHRISTIAN LIBERTY

Donald Grey Barnhouse, the former pastor of Tenth Presbyterian Church in Philadelphia, was once traveling on a train. During his travel, he opened his Bible and spent time studying it. A young student was sitting across the aisle, reading a magazine. Noticing Dr. Barnhouse, he walked up to him and asked him how he could be a man of the Word and know the Bible. Dr. Barnhouse replied, "Son, as long as you continue to read those magazines more than you read this Book, you will know more about those magazines than you do about this Book."[3]

JOSH MCDOWELL'S GUIDE TO UNDERSTANDING YOUR BIBLE

God's Word only works its true blessing when the truth it brings to us has stirred *the inner life*, and reproduced itself in resolve, trust, love, or adoration. When the heart has received the Word through the mind, and has had its spiritual powers called out and exercised on it, the Word is no longer void, but has done that which God sent it to do. It has become part of our life, and strengthened us for new purpose and effort. It is through meditation that the heart holds and appropriates the Word. Just as in reflecting on the Bible, the understanding grasps all the meaning and bearings of a truth, so in meditation, the heart assimilates it and makes it a part of its own life. Remember that when we speak of the heart, we mean the will and the affection. The meditation of the heart implies desire, acceptance, surrender, love. . . . The intellect gathers and prepares the food on which we are to feed. In meditation the heart takes it in and feeds on it. The art of meditation needs to be cultivated. Just as a person needs to be trained to concentrate his mental powers in order to think clearly and accurately, a Christian needs to carefully consider and meditate, until the holy habit has been formed of yielding up the whole heart to every word of God. . . . Meditation is the heart turning towards God with His own Word, seeking to take it into the affection and will, into its very life.[4]

ANDREW MURRAY IN THE INNER LIFE

ENJOY HIS PRESENCE

Choose one verse from today's study and make it your focus as you go about your day. You might write it out on a three-by-five card, read through it during the day, and consider memorizing it.

REST IN HIS LOVE

"The unfolding of Your words gives light; it gives understanding to the simple" (Psalm 119:130).

Dear Friend,

You have spent a lot of time this week looking at verses in Psalm 119 to learn about the magnificence of God's Word. It is the path to revival. Hold it reverently in your own life. Always remember this one great truth: behind the Word is God Himself. You are never alone when you read His Word. You might just take some time these last two days to read through Psalm 119 at one sitting, as though you were reading a prayer by a devout man of God.

What were your most meaningful discoveries this week as you spent time with the Lord?
Most meaningful insight:

Most meaningful devotional reading:

Most meaningful verse:

In the moments of our bitterest sorrow, how are we compelled to stand amazed at the tenderness, which is daily and hourly exercised towards us! We have always some word exactly suited to our affliction and which we could not have understood without it; and "a word thus spoken in due season, how good is it!" One word of God, sealed to the heart, infuses more sensible relief, than ten thousand words of man. . . . This indeed was the end, for which the Scriptures were written (Romans 15:4); and such power of consolation have they sometimes administered to the afflicted saint, that tribulation almost ceased to be a trial, and the retrospect has been the source of thankful recollection. But first the word becomes life—then comfort. And those only, who have felt the quickening power of the word, can realize its consolations.[1]

CHARLES BRIDGES IN HIS COMMENTARY, PSALM 119

preparation for revival

week
six

PSALM 119:143

under His mighty hand

My soul cleaves to the dust;
Revive me according to Your word.
PSALM 119:25

Prepare Your Heart

There is an element of mystery in the Christian life. It is that span between God's ways and man's ways in everyday affairs. At times, things don't go our way or in the direction we think is best. The mystery enters because of the facts of God: He is good, His ways are just, He is sovereign, He never makes a mistake. These are things that cannot be shaken. They are true.

Yet at times, life takes such turns that it seems to oppose everything we know is true about God. Therein lies the mystery. Whatever has happened, God remains true and has not changed. These are the things that prepare our hearts for God's Spirit to breathe in us the winds of revival. Never does the ground of our hearts become more ready to receive the Word of God as when we come to this point in life.

Perhaps that is why the greatest works have come from seasons of adversity. Those men and women who have been used mightily by God have walked a road of deep suffering. In their suffering, they have held fast to God, even if by a thread. To persevere in the trial and to agonize at times with the truth of God's Word always means walking the road of humility, the Cross, brokenness, confession and repentance, and surrender.

The author of Psalm 119 was well acquainted with suffering. He saw it as the classroom where he learned to walk with God. There his priorities and commitments were forged. In the same way, God has called you to the highest and the best: an abundant, victorious life lived in intimacy with Him. He will refresh and renew you day by day with rivers of living water. You will know what it is to have true meaning in life as you live out what God has planned for you. The times of suffering that crash in uninvited will prepare your heart to receive the things of God in a new and deeper way.

As you begin this week of quiet times, ask the Lord to give you the grace to respond to Him in ways that will prepare the ground of your heart to receive His Word. Ask Him to teach you the value of humility, the Cross, brokenness, confession and repentance, and surrender. Write a brief prayer to the Lord as a preparation of heart today.

READ AND STUDY GOD'S WORD

1. You have had the opportunity in these last few weeks to think about the life situation of the author of Psalm 119. By way of review, look at the following verses in Psalm 119 to think more deeply about his life experience. As you look at each verse, describe the depth of his suffering in your own words.

verse 25

verse 28

verse 107

verse 141

verse 143

verse 161

verse 176

2. First Peter is a letter about suffering, our response to it, and its value in the life of the believer. Look at the following passages in 1 Peter and record your insights about suffering.

   1:3-7

   2:13-25

   3:1-9

   3:13-17

   4:12-19

   5:6-10

3. Summarize what you have learned about suffering. What should be your response to it?

4. What do you think it means to be "under the mighty hand of God" (1 Peter 5:6)?

5. The word *humble* in the Greek is in the passive voice and, according to Kenneth Wuest, means that the subject of the verb is passive in the hands of God and is acted

upon by Him.[1] What will it take for you to humble yourself under God's mighty hand?

ADORE GOD IN PRAYER

What experiences are bringing you to a place of humility? Turn to your Prayer Pages and write out the burdens of your heart. Place each of these things in the Lord's hands. Ask the Lord to work something miraculous and mighty according to His own purposes in each thing you have given Him.

YIELD YOURSELF TO GOD

The exhortation is *Be humbled* or *Suffer yourselves to be humbled* [1 Peter 5:6]. The humbling process which God was using was the persecution and suffering through which these Christians were passing. Peter exhorts these believers to react towards these in a God-honoring way, to be submissive to the discipline which God was using to make them more humble. But with this exhortation comes also a note of comfort and hope in that the presence of humility in the life of a Christian is the prerequisite that God demands before He will exalt that Christian to a high place of privilege and honor in His service. As someone has said, "He must take a low place before God, who would take a high place before men."[2]

KENNETH WUEST IN *WUEST'S WORD STUDIES*

My brother and sister, you who have been admitted into the school of suffering, you who have been cast into the fires of purification, and who feel the pain thereof both in soul and in body, do not become discouraged. Above all, do not murmur against God! I know you are tempted to do this when your suffering seems unendurable, but do not murmur. Rather pray God that you may be given grace to be still. For something great is taking place in your life. God is working in your inner life and effecting your sanctification. He is purging away the dross in order that He may imprint His own image upon you, the quiet and lowly image of Him in His suffering, which cannot be impressed upon us except by suffering. He Himself learned obedience by the things which He suffered (Hebrews 5:7-8). Can we then very well expect to learn obedience in some other easier way? If you think at any time that your sufferings are too great, too heavy to bear, then turn your tear-filled eyes unto Jesus. Remember Him in His sufferings, and pray the Holy Spirit to reveal Christ unto you. Pray, not only that you may hold out in your sufferings, but also that you may see God in them.[3]

O. HALLESBY IN *UNDER HIS WINGS*

It is the meek man who never turns aside from the purpose of God. Show me a man who will make up his mind about something, set to work, and patiently take all the rebuffs and knocks, the criticism and unkindness, and that man will never give in. He will finish that which he began because he possesses the grace of perseverance.[4]

ALAN REDPATH IN *FAITH FOR THE TIMES*

ENJOY HIS PRESENCE

Annie Johnson Flint, author of six thousand hymns, understood suffering. She was an orphan, lived with crippling arthritis, and was stricken with cancer. Yet listen to these words that she has written. Hear the overcoming spirit within and the eternal perspective that God is at work in a powerful way.

It is the branch that bears the fruit,
That feels the knife
To prune it for a larger growth,
A fuller life.
Though every budding twig be lopped,
And every grace
Of swaying tendril, springing leaf,
Be lost a space,
O thou whose life of joy seems reft,
Of beauty shorn;
Whose aspirations lie in dust,
All bruised and torn,
Rejoice, tho' each desire, each dream,
Each hope of thine
Shall fall and fade; it is the hand
Of Love Divine
That holds the knife, that cuts and breaks
With tenderest touch,
That thou, whose life has borne some fruit
May'st now bear much.[5]

Jesus said in John 15:2, "Every branch that bears fruit, He prunes it so that it may bear more fruit." Even the deepest darknesses of life that sometimes occur after a period of fruitfulness can result in something that brings honor to the name of Christ.

REST IN HIS LOVE

"God disciplines us for our good, that we may share in his holiness" (Hebrews 12:10, NIV).

the cross

I am exceedingly afflicted;
Revive me, O LORD, according to Your word.
PSALM 119:107

Prepare Your Heart

Two thousand years ago, Jesus Christ was executed on a cross. In those days, many people were crucified. It was a death designed for the worst criminals, but certainly undeserved for the sinless Creator of the universe. Why was the Son of God crucified, and what place does the Cross now have in the lives of His followers? Today you will think about the Cross of Jesus Christ and its meaning in your life.

One cannot consider suffering and preparation for revival without thinking about the Cross. In the Cross we see death. In the natural world, life leads to death, but in the spiritual world, death leads to life. It is a different kind of death. It is death to self and to sin. Then comes eternal life, made possible by Christ's death. Ask God to open your eyes in a new way today to the meaning of the Cross of Christ in your life.

The Old Rugged Cross

On a hill far away stood an old rugged cross,
the emblem of suffering and shame;
and I love that old cross where the dearest and best
for a world of lost sinners was slain.

Refrain:

So I'll cherish the old rugged cross,
till my trophies at last I lay down;
I will cling to the old rugged cross,
and exchange it some day for a crown.

O that old rugged cross, so despised by the world,
has a wondrous attraction for me;
for the dear Lamb of God left his glory above
to bear it to dark Calvary.

Refrain

In that old rugged cross, stained with blood so divine,
a wondrous beauty I see,
for 'twas on that old cross Jesus suffered and died,
to pardon and sanctify me.

Refrain

To that old rugged cross I will ever be true,
its shame and reproach gladly bear;
then he'll call me some day to my home far away,
where his glory forever I'll share.

Refrain

GEORGE BENNARD (1873–1958)

READ AND STUDY GOD'S WORD

The psalmist of Psalm 119 was "exceedingly afflicted" (verse 107). His affliction caused him
to turn to God and pray for revival. When suffering goes beyond difficult to seemingly
impossible, we fall at the Lord's feet in submission and humility. That is what the Cross does
when it is at work in your life. The Cross takes us from death to life, from the world to God,
from sin to holiness. It calls us to say no to the world and yes to God. The ongoing work of
the Cross brings us to the choice of casting ourselves upon the Lord. Suffering is often the
tool God uses to turn our eyes away from ourselves and onto Him. In the Cross there is
always humility, laying aside of rights and privileges, and total abandonment to God.

1. Look at the following passages and record what you learn about the Cross. How do
these words apply to your life today? Personalize your insights and responses.
Matthew 16:24-26

John 12:24-26

Romans 6:6-11

Galatians 2:19-20

1 Peter 2:24

2. Summarize what you have learned about the Cross from these verses.

3. What does the Cross mean for you in your life today?

4. Read Philippians 2:5-11. What do you learn about Christ? What did it take for Christ to go to the cross? Record your insights.

5. What is bringing you to the Cross today? What in your life causes you to turn away from yourself and run to God?

6. What things in your life is the Lord asking you to die to that you might say yes to Him?

Are you willing to lay these things aside to follow Him? Are you willing to participate in the plans and purposes of God even if you do not understand the path where He has led?

ADORE GOD IN PRAYER

Today pray, *Revive my heart, O Lord.* In your trials, continue to ask the Lord to revive you.

YIELD YOURSELF TO GOD

The Cross of Jesus Christ stands unique and alone. His cross is not our cross. Our cross is that we manifest before the world the fact that we are sanctified to do nothing but the will of God. By means of His cross, our cross becomes our divinely appointed privilege.[1]

OSWALD CHAMBERS IN *CHRISTIAN DISCIPLINE*

The production of a saint is the grandest thing earth can give to heaven. A saint is not a person with a saintly character: a saint is a saintly character. Character, not ecstatic moods, is the stuff of saintliness. A saint is a living epistle written by the finger of God, known and read of all people. A saint may be any person, any wastrel or vagabond, who discovering himself at Calvary, with the nature of sin uncloaked, lies in despair; then discerning Jesus Christ as the substitute for sin and rising in the glamour of amazement, he cries out: "Jesus, I should be there." And to his astonished spirit, he receives justification from all his sinfulness by that wondrous atonement. Then, standing in that great light, and placing his hands, as it were, over his Savior's crucified hands, his feet over His crucified feet, he crucifies forever his right to himself. And the Lord baptizes him with the Holy Spirit and fire; substituting in him a new principles of life, and identity of holiness with Himself, until he bears unmistakably a family likeness to Jesus Christ.[2]

OSWALD CHAMBERS IN *CHRISTIAN DISCIPLINE*

Enjoy His Presence

Jesus, Keep Me Near the Cross

Jesus, keep me near the cross;
there a precious fountain, free to all,
a healing stream,
flows from Calvary's mountain.

Refrain:
In the cross, in the cross,
be my glory ever,
till my raptured soul shall find
rest beyond the river.

Near the cross, a trembling soul,
love and mercy found me;
there the bright and morning star
sheds its beams around me.

Refrain

Near the cross! O Lamb of God,
bring its scenes before me;
help me walk from day to day
with its shadow o'er me.

Refrain

Fanny Crosby

Rest in His Love

"Those who belong to Christ Jesus have crucified the sinful nature with its passions and
desires. Since we live by the Spirit, let us keep in step with the Spirit" (Galatians 5:24-25, NIV).

brokenness

My soul weeps because of grief;
Strengthen me according to Your word.
PSALM 119:28

Prepare Your Heart

What is the best preparation for a heart to overflow with rivers of living water from the Holy Spirit? Brokenness. The broken heart recognizes its need for God. It knows there is nothing that will meet its need except God. It recognizes its true place before God. It is emptied of everything but God. It is yielded, humble, and submitted to God. This is the heart God can revive.

As a preparation of heart, meditate on Psalm 34. Choose the verse that is most significant to you today and write it out in your Journal. Write two to three sentences about why this verse is significant. Complete your Journal writing with a prayer to the Lord.

READ AND STUDY GOD'S WORD

1. Every man or woman of God has experienced brokenness in his or her life. The Bible is filled with experiences of brokenness. The Lord meets His own in the midst of their condition. For example, Hagar was Sarah's Egyptian maid. Sarah wanted children so much that she had forced Hagar to have a son with Abraham. In the end, Sarah was so resentful of Hagar that she sent her away, along with her son, to the wilderness of Beersheba. Read Genesis 21:9-21. What do you observe about Hagar's brokenness and how God met her in her brokenness?

2. What can you know about brokenness? Read the following verses and record your insights.

Psalm 34:18

Psalm 147:3

Matthew 5:3-4

Revelation 21:4

3. Jeremiah was known as the weeping prophet. He was one of the Lord's choice servants who knew what it was to be broken. Read Jeremiah 8:18–9:2. What caused Jeremiah to be broken?

4. Describe what you think it means to be broken before the Lord.

ADORE GOD IN PRAYER

Help me, O Lord, to believe that what seems to be my losses are really gains and that each ounce of suffering is adding to the weight of glory, not only after this life, but also now.[1]

F. B. MEYER IN *DAILY PRAYERS*

YIELD YOURSELF TO GOD

God's purpose is to break our will, not our spirit. His purpose is not to destroy us, but to bring us to a position of maximum wholeness, maturity, and usefulness in His kingdom. He wants us to yield control of our lives to Him. The last thing in the world that Peter wanted to give up was control. He wanted to dictate whether his feet would be washed, the terms by which he would prove Jesus was indeed walking on the water, the way Jesus was going to become the Messiah. We are like Peter—each one of us has a very difficult time giving up control. We always want to have the final say. Brokenness is God's process of bringing us to the point where we not only don't have the final say, we have nothing to say, except to ask, "Lord Jesus, what would you have me to do?"[2]

CHARLES STANLEY IN *THE BLESSINGS OF BROKENNESS*

The first thing God does with us is to get us based on rugged Reality until we do not care what becomes of us individually as long as He gets His way for the purpose of His Redemption. Why shouldn't we go through heartbreaks? Through those doorways God is opening up ways of fellowship with His Son. Most of us fall and collapse at the first grip of pain; we sit down on the threshold of God's purpose and die away of self-pity, and all so called Christian sympathy will aid us to our death bed. But God will not. He comes with the grip of the pierced hand of His Son, and says—"Enter into fellowship with Me; arise and shine." If through a broken heart God can bring His purposes to pass in the world, then thank Him for breaking your heart.[3]

OSWALD CHAMBERS IN *MY UTMOST FOR HIS HIGHEST*

ENJOY HIS PRESENCE

Are you familiar with the life of brokenness? God is near the brokenhearted. Brokenness makes way for the blessing of revival. Never is your heart more prepared for God and His Word than when it is broken.

> Lord, when I think I cannot stand,
> that's when you hold me in your hand.
> And when confusion blinds my way,
> then on your words my heart will stay.

When the enemy seems to bind me,
only then can you refine me.[4]

Debra Collins

Rest in His Love
"The LORD is close to the brokenhearted and saves those who are crushed in spirit. A righteous man may have many troubles, but the LORD delivers him from them all" (Psalm 34:18-19, NIV).

confession and repentance

I have gone astray like a lost sheep; seek Your servant,
For I do not forget Your commandments.
PSALM 119:176

Prepare Your Heart

Augustine of Hippo was born in North Africa in A.D. 354. His father was a pagan, but his mother was a devout Christian. Leaning more toward his father's ways, Augustine gave in to his passions and had a mistress who bore him a son. He studied rhetoric at Carthage and taught in Rome and then Milan. In Milan he met Ambrose, whose preaching was of such power that Augustine had to consider the truths of Christ. As a result, he became a Christian.

Augustine's most famous work is *The Confessions*. His words penetrate the soul as he recounts God's works and his own sin. He addresses the questions that stir in the human heart as he recounts his struggles and search for God. *The Confessions* depicts the soul's journey to the grace of God.

In the brokenness and humility that lead to personal spiritual revival, one becomes painfully aware of personal sin. Never is God's holiness so apparent as when a heart is yielded in submission to God. And what is a believer to do about the sin in his or her life? First John 1:9 says, "If we confess our sins, He is faithful and righteous to forgive us our sins and to cleanse us from all unrighteousness."

Turn to Isaiah 53 as a preparation of heart for your time with the Lord today. These words describe Jesus, who fulfilled this prophecy of the One who would come as the Suffering Servant. In what ways did He deal with our sorrow and sin? Personalize your observations as you look at these verses (for example, "He bore *my* griefs").

171

READ AND STUDY GOD'S WORD

1. The author of Psalm 119 was acutely aware of his own sin. In fact, because of his love for God and His Word, he desired to be holy before God and to honor Him in everything he did. Look at these verses in Psalm 119 and note what you see about the author's view of sin.

verses 9-11

verses 34-36

verses 59-60

verse 67

verse 133

verse 176

2. Describe the author's attitude toward sin.

3. What kind of response to sin honors God? David was a man after God's own heart, who also became entangled in sin. Read the account of his sin in 2 Samuel 11:1–12:25. What do you see in his response that honored God?

4. Read Psalm 51. This is the prayer of confession that David wrote after his sin with Bathsheba. After reading this psalm, what do you think it means to confess and repent of your sin?

ADORE GOD IN PRAYER

Has God revealed any unconfessed sin or area of unbelief in your own life today? If so, bring your sin to the Lord, who promises that when you do, He is faithful to forgive your sin and cleanse you from unrighteousness (see 1 John 1:9). Write a prayer in your Journal, confessing any sin or unbelief to the Lord, and then ask Him to fill you with His Holy Spirit.

Personal spiritual revival is a constant renewal of God's purpose in your life and a deepening of your devotion to Him and intimacy with Him. In real and tangible ways, God restores and transforms you. Because He has revived you, you are able to live with the "roof off" and the "walls down" in your relationship with Him and others. No masks. No secret life. Instead, your life is open to God, and your heart is vulnerable to Him so that you may be touched and moved and changed by the Holy Spirit.

YIELD YOURSELF TO GOD

Alas, what bruises have come to your life and mine because of sin! But here is One who stands beside us. He has no bruise or weakness, and from His position of power and perfection He can tell us that there is no life so bruised that need be utterly broken, there are none so injured in life who cannot be healed, or so depraved that they cannot be transformed. There is no man so far from God that the blood of the Lord Jesus Christ cannot bring him near. No individual anywhere has been so gripped by sin that he cannot be set free and wrenched clear; for the virus of any sin, no matter how deep, can be cleansed and cured through the blood of the Lord Jesus Christ. A bruised reed He will not break, but by His grace and power, in love and mercy, He will restore, renew, and re-impower. I wonder if I speak to a bruised reed. Let me tell you there is no one beyond the reach of the Saviour's love, no one beyond the reach of His pardon. He looks upon the tremendous bulk of the sin of the whole world, and because He is without bruises and is no mere smoking flax, but burns as a living flame, He is able to cast all that mountain of sin into the depths of the sea.[1]

ALAN REDPATH IN *FAITH FOR THE TIMES*

Those whom God uses in leadership in revival are always men who have met with God in a powerfully personal way and have a burning passion for the glory of God and a life of holiness. It is not possible for the Holy Spirit to come in great power upon his people without creating a longing for right and pure living.[2]

BRIAN EDWARDS IN *REVIVAL: A PEOPLE SATURATED WITH GOD*

ENJOY HIS PRESENCE

C. S. Lewis said that our very dissatisfaction with the temporal proves we were made for the eternal. We are like fish out of water. Just as the fish is out of its element when out of water, so are we when disconnected from the eternal. Our home is heaven with all its glory and beauty.

God's design is perfection. Flawlessness. Nothing less. And nowhere does He desire this perfection more than in us. We are designed to be visions of beauty, created by God. If we are created for heaven, then we must act like it.

One of God's great purposes for us is purity. It means to be stainless, spotless, unmixed with any matter. In the Old Testament, the word *zakkah* means to be clean, innocent, transparent, and clear.[3] In the New Testament, the word for pure is *hagnos* and means to be chaste and undefiled. Something is going to happen at the end of time, when God ushers you into eternity. He will present you as the bride for His Son, Jesus Christ. And as a Christian, you are united with Christ even now. What is significant about your intimate relationship with Christ? He is the King of kings. He is the unblemished Lamb who sacrificed Himself to pay the penalty for your sins, that you might be washed clean of every sin—past, present, and future. His death accomplished everything necessary to make you the person He wants you to be. Because He is holy, He will never be satisfied with less than purity in you.

Perhaps you have tried to be perfect, and failed. Purity is not something that you achieve on your own. It is something God does within you once and for all, with ongoing, moment-by-moment results until you step into eternity. That is where personal revival by God through His Word and the Holy Spirit is so essential. Honesty with yourself and God about your sin is essential because, as Corrie ten Boom said, "The blood of Christ never cleansed any excuses, only sin." His is an offer of love and forgiveness if you will only run to Him.

God wants your holiness even more than your happiness. One may be happy in a temporal way and skip merrily toward the fires of hell. That is not what God has in mind for you. God desires you to have the highest and the best.

The author of Psalm 119 desired purity in his own life. "How can a young man keep his way pure?" the psalmist asked. "By keeping it according to Your word" (verse 9). Jesus said, "You are already clean because of the word which I have spoken to you" (John 15:3). In revival, we need the cleansing work of the Word of God by the power of the Holy Spirit. This cleansing brings about a purity that shines like a brilliant diamond from within. That is why Paul said to the Philippian church, "Do all things without grumbling or disputing; so that you will prove yourselves to be blameless and innocent, children of God above reproach in the midst of a crooked and perverse generation, among whom you appear as lights in the world, holding fast the word of life, so that in the day of Christ I will have reason to glory because I did not run in vain nor toil in vain" (Philippians 2:14-16). As you close your quiet time today, remember to keep your eyes on Him. Desire holiness much more than happiness. Then shine for Him in the midst of a world that is, more and more, becoming a lover of self and pleasure rather than a lover of God (see 2 Timothy 3:1-5).

Lord Jesus, how I thank Thee that Thou hast not only redeemed me with Thy precious blood, reconciled me to God and established peace between my guilty soul and God my Maker, but I thank Thee that Thou art risen from the dead, that at this very moment Thou dost indwell me in the person and power of Thy divine Spirit; that Thou hast never expected of me anything but failure, yet Thou hast given to me Thy strength for my weakness, Thy victory for my defeat, Thyself for all my bankruptcy! I step out now by faith, into a future that is limited only by what Thou art! To me to live is Christ! For Thy Name's sake, Amen.[4]

MAJOR W. IAN THOMAS IN THE SAVING LIFE OF CHRIST

REST IN HIS LOVE

"If we confess our sins, He is faithful and righteous to forgive us our sins and to cleanse us from all unrighteousness" (1 John 1:9).

surrender

You are good and do good:
Teach me Your statutes.
PSALM 119:68

Trouble and anguish have come upon me,
Yet Your commandments are my delight.
PSALM 119:143

Prepare Your Heart

There is a time in every believer's life when he or she is brought to a place of decision with God. It is a decision to trust God no matter what. This decision involves placing one's whole self in God's hands. This act is called consecration or surrender. It is the point when the believer decides to step over the line, hold nothing back, and go with God. It is a reckless abandonment to the will of God. Once you have stepped over the line, you are the Lord's radicle disciple. You will live on the edge of your faith in a way you never have before. Then your life will influence the world.

Does such surrender come easily? No. The way to it is paved with humility, brokenness, confession and repentance, and the Cross. Such graces are gifts from God. The result is personal spiritual revival.

Are you wrestling with anything in your own life today? If so, perhaps that is the very circumstance God is using to bring you to a place of surrender to Him.

Surrender is something we resist all of our lives. But without surrender to God, we cannot be transformed. When you surrender to God, you place yourself in the hands of the Master Potter. He has a beautiful vessel in mind and will proceed to make you the person He wants you to be. Today you will think about what it will take to surrender to God, like clay in the Potter's hands.

As you begin your time with the Lord, turn to Psalm 111. Read through this psalm and then list everything you learn about the Lord. Ask God to speak to you today as you study His Word.

READ AND STUDY GOD'S WORD

1. Read Romans 12:1-2. Describe what God wants you to do. What do you think He means when He says to "present your bodies a living and holy sacrifice, acceptable to God"? How does this help you understand what it means to surrender to God?

2. What did surrender to God involve for the following servants of God? In what ways did these circumstances humble and break them, and bring about God's magnificent plan?
    Abraham in Genesis 22:1-19

    Moses in Exodus 3–4

    Jesus in John 12:23-33; Luke 22:39-44

3. According to the following passages, what does it mean that we are like clay in the Potter's hand? Record your insights.
    Isaiah 29:13-16

Isaiah 45:5-12

Isaiah 64:8-9

Jeremiah 18:1-6

ADORE GOD IN PRAYER

Thank the Lord today for those circumstances that have brought you to a place of trust and surrender to Him. Confess every sin and lay aside anything that would hinder you from following Jesus Christ with all your heart, soul, mind, and strength.

YIELD YOURSELF TO GOD

> To yield does involve a giving up but it means giving up what really is not yours; it means giving up something only to get something of infinitely greater worth; yes, it means giving up something that He needs for His use to the One we love best; more than all it means giving up something to the One who loves us with a love so great that He died for us and now waits to bestow upon us all the exhaustless treasure that are ours in Him. Can we not trust "the Man who died for us?" . . . Surrender taken alone is a plunge into a cold void. When it is a surrender to the Son of God who loved me and gave Himself for me it is the bright home coming of the soul to the seat and sphere of life and power.[1]

RUTH PAXSON IN LIFE ON THE HIGHEST PLANE

This is your hour. You know enough now to act upon. You know Christ as your Saviour; He comes and claims to be your Lord. He is your safety; He wants to be your satisfaction; He is your righteousness; He wants to be your holiness. He wants to lead you on and lead you out and lead you up. Cannot you trust Him? Won't you go with Him? *Will a man rob God?* As a blood-bought and blood-washed soul, I have no further right to myself; I have no right to do what I like, to go where I like, to be what I like, to say what I like, to read what I like, to form companionships I like, to choose the career I like. I handed myself over in that great hour of my regeneration to Jesus Christ, and I belong to Him by every right—creation, preservation, and redemption; and unless you can give a reason to the Risen Christ tonight for not surrendering yourself absolutely to Him, you have got to do it.[2]

REV. W. GRAHAM SCROGGIE IN "NOW, THEN DO IT" FROM KESWICK'S AUTHENTIC VOICE

When a man sees with His soul the truth of what I have been saying to you, there suddenly bursts out of the night of his experience a shout of praise, a song of rejoicing, music and melody in his soul. What has made the praise, and what has caused him to rejoice? Simply this: he has believed the promise of our text (Isaiah 41:10): "Fear thou not; for I am with thee"—not intellectually, but with a total commitment which has enabled him to lie down upon it. He has discovered, for the first time in his life, that every shattering experience that has happened to him has been focused to this one objective: to bring him to the place where he lies down in God. Faith is conscious that God is there, and faith knows that His presence is the answer and the complement of every need. So the little desert bush of his life begins to glow and burn with reality that He is in him. Faith recognizes that God has entered into a covenant with His Son, sealed by His precious blood, which can never be dissolved. His faithfulness and love are bound to finish the task in a man's life which He has begun. Faith knows that behind the chastening, the suffering, and the trial, behind that restriction of circumstance, there is a great purpose. The great Refiner of hearts has a meaning in every degree of heat which He allows the furnace to have.[3]

ALAN REDPATH IN FAITH FOR THE TIMES

Faith in the Bible is faith in God against everything that contradicts Him—I will remain true to God's character whatever He may do. *Though He slay me, yet will I trust Him*—this is the most sublime utterance of faith in the whole of the Bible.[4]

OSWALD CHAMBERS IN MY UTMOST FOR HIS HIGHEST

Is there anything in your life that you have been wrestling with? In what way might God be using that very thing to bring you to a deeper surrender to Him where you can say with Job, "Though he slay me, yet will I hope in him" (Job 13:15, NIV)?

ENJOY HIS PRESENCE

> Take my life, and let it be consecrated, Lord, to thee.
> Take my moments and my days; let them flow in ceaseless praise.
> Take my hands, and let them move at the impulse of thy love.
> Take my feet, and let them be swift and beautiful for thee.
> Take my voice, and let me sing always, only, for my King.

Take my lips, and let them be filled with messages from thee.
Take my silver and my gold; not a mite would I withhold.
Take my intellect, and use every power as thou shalt choose.
Take my will, and make it thine; it shall be no longer mine.
Take my heart, it is thine own; it shall be thy royal throne.
Take my love, my Lord, I pour at thy feet its treasure-store.
Take myself, and I will be ever, only, all for thee.

FRANCES R. HAVERGAL

Have you ever said to Him, "Lord Jesus, I have only a very simple life to offer you as a dwelling place but while you are here *it is all yours*. Go where you want to, do what you want to—*just make yourself at home!*" He waits for just such an invitation. How quickly He will accept it when once honestly offered and how He will spread out over the whole life—truly making Himself at home. If you have not unlocked all the doors from the inside and given Him a gracious and glad invitation to enter, will you do so today?[5]

RUTH PAXSON IN LIFE ON THE HIGHEST PLANE

REST IN HIS LOVE
"Though he slay me, yet will I hope in him" (Job 13:15, NIV).

DEAR FRIEND,

In what ways do you think God prepared the psalmist's heart for revival? In what ways is God preparing you for personal spiritual revival?

What were your most meaningful discoveries this week as you spent time with the Lord? Most meaningful insight:

Most meaningful devotional reading:

Most meaningful verse:

God reads the heart, and unless we fear God and sin above all else, we cannot expect his Spirit in revival. There can be no point in seeking revival for the church, and its benefit for the nation, until we are prepared and longing for revival in our own lives. And if God has used leaders to prepare the way for his Spirit in the past, where are those leaders today? Where are the men who are humble and broken before God, men who are longing for God beyond all else, and men who ache with a longing for God to get glory to himself and saturate the community with his presence? And where are the men with courage and determination to lead the church forward and never to give up the vision of what God can do?[1]

BRIAN EDWARDS IN *REVIVAL: A PEOPLE SATURATED WITH GOD*

the prayer of revival

week
seven

PSALM 119:149

the radical response of prayer

Oh that my ways may be established
To keep Your statutes!
PSALM 119:5

Prepare Your Heart

There is a day when God begins to shake the heart of His servant who has been broken of the self-life and is surrendered to God. That shaking leads to a bold and courageous move that impacts the world. The servant of God is burdened with a tremendous desire to pray. The servant does not always realize the result. Sometimes heaven is the greatest witness to what happens when one person, moved by God, begins to pray. Only at the throne of God is the true impact of prayer realized.

Prayer is like incense rising up to God's throne (see Revelation 8:3). He hears your prayer. This is the great motivation to pray. He loves you with an everlasting love—unconditional, kind, compassionate, and sacrificial. He holds you in the palm of His hand. When you pray, He is moved. And when God is moved, things happen.

God has a plan and a purpose. He carries out that plan and purpose in a magnificent way that brings great glory to Him. Through prayer, you join God in His work in the world. He designed things such that you are involved in something greater than yourself because He is the One doing the work.

This week you will look at what happens to the prayers of one who experiences personal spiritual revival. Something changes. God can work amazing things through the prayers of one who has turned to Him in brokenness and surrender. As you begin this day with the Lord, write a prayer in your Journal, expressing all that is on your heart. Think about your life of prayer. Ask the Lord to work something new and powerful in your prayers.

READ AND STUDY GOD'S WORD

1. Turn to Psalm 119:1-5. What inspired such an incredible prayer by this psalmist, who was experiencing extreme difficulty? What is the psalmist thinking about?

2. The Word of God prompted prayer in the life of this man in difficult circumstances. He cried out to God. What did he cry out in verses 5-8?

3. King David told the Lord that he wanted to build Him a temple. The Lord's words in response to this request motivated David to pray. What do you learn about prayer from 2 Samuel 7?

4. Why do you think God's Word prompts a person to pray? What is it about the Word that causes a heart to turn to God?

ADORE GOD IN PRAYER

My Father God, enable me to roll my ways onto you, to trust you, and to believe that when I stand with you in the perfect daylight, I will see and understand those things that now I take on trust. All your ways are mercy and truth.[1]

F. B. MEYER IN *DAILY PRAYERS*

YIELD YOURSELF TO GOD

Prayer opens the way for the Word of God to run without hindrance. It creates the atmosphere that is favorable for the Word to accomplish its purpose. Prayer puts wheels under God's Word and gives wings to the angel of the Lord *having the everlasting gospel to preach unto them that dwell on the earth, and to every nation, and kindred, and tongue, and people* (Rev. 14:6). . . . Prayer exalts the Word of God and gives it preeminence in those who faithfully and wholeheartedly call upon the name of the Lord. Prayer draws its very life from the Bible. It places its security on the firm ground of Scripture. Its very existence and character depend on revelation made by God to man in His holy Word. Prayer, in turn, exalts this same revelation and turns men toward that Word. The nature, necessity, and all-comprehending character of prayer are based on the Word of God.[2]

E. M. BOUNDS IN *E.M. BOUNDS ON PRAYER*

If we are to obtain from God all that we ask from Him, Christ's words must abide or continue in us. We must study His words, fairly devour His words, let them sink into our thought and into our heart, keep them in our memory, obey them constantly in our life, let them shape and mold our daily life and our every act.[3]

R. A. TORREY IN *HOW TO PRAY*

ENJOY HIS PRESENCE
Has God been shaking your heart in such a way that you sense His call to pray? Will you resolve to grow in your life of prayer? Write down what you desire to see happen in your prayers.

REST IN HIS LOVE
"Now He was telling them a parable to show that at all times they ought to pray and not to lose heart" (Luke 18:1).

the prayer of resolve and commitment

I shall delight in Your commandments,
Which I love.
And I shall lift up my hands to Your commandments,
Which I love;
And I will meditate on Your statutes.
PSALM 119:47-48

Prepare Your Heart

Most people know about the influence of Evan Roberts in the Welsh Revival. Very few know about another man who was just as significant in this great revival. Norman Grubb shares this man's story in *Rees Howells: Intercessor.* Just before the Welsh Revival, Rees Howells was in America seeking his fortune. His heart, however, was seeking something of far greater worth: the Lord Jesus Christ. Once he realized he needed to know God, he searched daily for five months for the way to God. He said he would have gladly paid all the money he possessed if only he could find a man to show him the way to eternal life.

One day he attended a meeting led by a man named Maurice Reuben. Afterward, Howells recalled,

It seemed as if I spent ages at the Savior's feet, and I wept and wept. I felt as if He had died just for me. I lost myself. I had been living in the fear of death, and I saw Him taking that death for me. My parents loved me very much and, up to that time, to me there were no people like them, but they never suffered death for me. He *did* it. His love for me, as compared with theirs, was as high as the heavens above the earth, and He won my love—every bit of it. He broke me, and everything in me went right out to Him.[1]

Howells said that the day of his new birth in Jesus Christ was the most outstanding day

191

of his life. As soon as he came to know Christ, he was compelled to return to his homeland of Wales. Only God could have so strategically worked together such a series of events. His return occurred in 1904, the time of the revival. So many came to know Christ during this time that there were not enough mature believers to nurture them in their newfound faith. The need arose for intercessors, willing to pray for those new believers. Rees Howells was God's chosen man for that ministry.

When God called Howells to intercede for others, he resolved to become a prayer warrior. As God showed him new things about prayer, Howells immediately resolved to do what God said. The results were exciting. One day, God moved Howells to pray for a man he knew named Jim Stakes, an alcoholic who lived in poverty. That evening there was a knock on Howells' door. It was Jim Stakes! He said he was in trouble because he was two years behind on his rent. Howells got the idea to pay one year's rent with his own money and raise the other year's rent from someone else. Then the Lord convicted him that he should pay the rent for both years. Immediately he resolved to do it. This act of kindness so moved Stakes that he committed his life to Christ. He asked Howells to visit his wife so that she might be saved as well. Thus, as a result of the commitments Howells came to in prayer, a downtrodden couple was able to come to know the love of Christ and to inherit eternal life.

God will show you many exciting truths in His Word. However, it is in prayer that those truths move you to a resolve and commitment to follow Christ. It is one thing to see words on a page but quite another to live by those words. In prayer you resolve to live one way or another, guided by the Holy Spirit according to the Word of God. Today ask God to show you what He wants you to resolve to do—such things as study His Word, obey His Word, speak the truth, pray for others, and love your neighbors.

READ AND STUDY GOD'S WORD

Two phrases that are repeated at least twenty times throughout Psalm 119 are "I will" and "I shall." This is the prayer of resolve and commitment. As this psalmist prays, the Lord moves him to become a man of conviction who resolves to do what pleases God.

1. Look at the following verses of Psalm 119 and record what the psalmist resolves to do.
   verses 7-8

   verses 15-16

   verse 32

verses 45-48

verse 62

verse 69

verse 93

verse 95

2. Josiah was a king who loved God. Read 2 Chronicles 34. What did Josiah resolve to do? What happened in his people's lives as a result?

3. Summarize what you have seen about resolve and commitment in prayer in the psalmist's life and in Josiah's life.

ADORE GOD IN PRAYER

As you think about those commitments that the psalmist of Psalm 119 and Josiah resolved to do in their life of prayer, which commitment speaks to your heart the most? Turn to your Journal and write a prayer of commitment related to that one thing that He lays on your heart.

YIELD YOURSELF TO GOD

Prayer governs conduct, and conduct makes character. Conduct is what we do. Character is what we are. Conduct is the outward life. Character is the unseen life, hidden within, yet is evidenced by that which is seen. Conduct is external, seen from without. Character is internal, operating within. In the economy of grace, conduct is the offspring of character. Character is the state of the heart. Conduct is its outward expression. Character is the root of the tree. Conduct is the fruit it bears. Prayer is related to all the gifts of grace. Its relationship to character and conduct is that of a helper. Prayer helps to establish character and to fashion conduct. Both, for their successful continuance, depend on prayer. There may be a certain degree of moral character and conduct independent of prayer, but there cannot be any distinctive religious character and Christian conduct without it. Prayer helps where all other aids fail. The more we pray, the better we are, and the purer and better our lives become.[2]

E. M. BOUNDS IN *E.M. BOUNDS ON PRAYER*

ENJOY HIS PRESENCE

Are your prayers filled with the same kind of resolve that you have seen in the lives of the psalmist and Josiah? Do you carry out in your life the things that you learn from the Lord in His Word? Ask the Lord today to remind you of this need for a resolute heart that makes commitments to Him as He reveals truth in His Word.

REST IN HIS LOVE

"Be earnest and unwearied and steadfast in your prayer life, being both alert and intent in your praying with thanksgiving" (Colossians 4:2, AMP).

intimate prayer

Blessed are You, O LORD.
PSALM 119:12

Prepare Your Heart

Jesus said to the church in Laodicea, "Behold, I stand at the door and knock; if anyone hears My voice and opens the door, I will come in to him and will dine with him, and he with Me" (Revelation 3:20). He says the same to Christians in every generation. Imagine sitting down and dining with Jesus, enjoying the sweet exchange that comes with a good meal and companionship with someone you love. Intimacy. That is what Jesus is inviting you to enjoy. Intimacy with Him.

The psalmist enjoyed this intimacy. Twenty-one times he said, "O LORD." There was an intimate knowing between his Lord and him. He said "O LORD" to that One whom he will recognize when he sees His Lord face to face in eternity.

Intimate prayer flows when God begins to quicken the heart and soul and restore a person to His purposes. Do you know this intimacy with the Lord? Today, ask the Lord for intimacy with Him. Meditate on the words of this Puritan prayer from *The Valley of Vision* as a preparation for your time alone with the Lord.

> God of my end,
> It is my greatest, noblest pleasure
> to be acquainted with thee
> and with my rational, immortal soul;
> It is sweet and entertaining
> to look into my being
> when all my powers and passions
> are united and engaged in pursuit of thee

when my soul longs and passionately breathes after conformity to thee
and the full enjoyment of thee;
No hours pass away with so much pleasure
as those spent in communion with thee
and with my heart.
O how desirable, how profitable to the Christian life
is a spirit of holy watchfulness
and godly jealousy over myself.
When my soul is afraid of nothing
except grieving and offending thee, the blessed God,
my Father and friend,
whom I then love and long to please,
rather than be happy in myself!
Knowing, as I do, that this is the pious temper,
worthy of the highest ambition, and closest pursuit
of intelligent creatures and holy Christians,
may my joy derive from glorifying and delighting thee.
I long to fill all my time for thee,
whether at home or in the way;
to place all my concerns in thy hands;
to be entirely at thy disposal,
having no will or interest of my own.
Help me to live to thee for ever,
to make thee my last and only end,
so that I may never more in one instance love my sinful self.[1]

READ AND STUDY GOD'S WORD

1. The writer of Psalm 119 addressed his Lord by saying "O LORD" in the following verses: 12, 31, 33, 41, 52, 55, 64-65, 75, 89, 107-108, 137, 145, 149, 151, 156, 159, 166, 169, and 174. In these words we see an intimate communion with the Lord. Look at the following occurrences and record the main topics of his prayer when he said, "O LORD." (If you have time, you may choose to look at the other verses that use this phrase.)

verses 64-65

verses 107-108

verse 166

verse 169

2. What do these verses and his words "O LORD" tell you about his relationship with the Lord?

3. John, one of Jesus' disciples, referred to himself as the one "whom Jesus loved." This phrase reveals the depth of intimacy with Jesus that every disciple may enjoy if he or she will pay the price in time and energy to know the Lord. Read John 13:1-30. What do you see in the relationship between Jesus and the one whom He loved?

4. When Jesus rose from the dead, He appeared to His disciples. Read John 21:1-7. What do you learn about John and his relationship with Jesus in this passage?

5. As an old man, John was exiled on the island of Patmos. There he received "The Revelation of Jesus Christ" (Revelation 1:1) and wrote about what he saw. Describe in your own words the vision of Jesus he recorded in Revelation 1:10-18.

ADORE GOD IN PRAYER

Have you loved the Lord in prayer? Have you simply sat in His presence in worship and adoration? Have you spoken intimately with Him, directing your words straight to His heart, as though you were looking into His eyes and calling Him by name: O Lord? Imagine that He is sitting here with you today (and He is). Talk openly with Him about whatever is on your heart, and be sure to repeat His name: Lord.

YIELD YOURSELF TO GOD

It would seem that admission to the inner circle of deepening intimacy with God is the outcome of *deep desire*. Only those who count such intimacy a prize worth sacrificing anything else for, are likely to attain it. If other intimacies are more desirable to us, we will not gain entry to that circle. The place on Jesus' breast is still vacant, and open to any who are willing to pay the price of deepening intimacy. We are now, and we will be in the future, only as intimate with God as we really choose to be.[2]

J. OSWALD SANDERS IN *ENJOYING INTIMACY WITH GOD*

ENJOY HIS PRESENCE

Close your time with the Lord by meditating on the words of this hymn by William Featherstone. If you know the music, you may wish to sing it to the Lord.

My Jesus, I love thee, I know thou art mine;
for thee all the follies of sin I resign.
My gracious Redeemer, my Savior art thou;
if ever I loved thee, my Jesus, 'tis now.

I love thee because thou hast first loved me,
and purchased my pardon on Calvary's tree;
I love thee for wearing the thorns on thy brow;
if ever I loved thee, my Jesus, 'tis now.

In mansions of glory and endless delight;
I'll ever adore thee in heaven so bright;
I'll sing with the glittering crown on my brow;
if ever I loved thee, my Jesus, 'tis now.

REST IN HIS LOVE

"I have loved you with an everlasting love; therefore I have drawn you with lovingkindness" (Jeremiah 31:3).

breakthrough prayer

Your hands made me and fashioned me;
Give me understanding that I may learn Your commandments.
PSALM 119:73

Prepare Your Heart

When God revives your heart as you pray, He will show you something new about Himself from His Word. This new truth will move you to pray for something new. In Psalm 119, this happens over and over again, showing us something incredible that happens when we pray. God breaks through the old things and reveals something new. It may be a new view of something you learned a long time ago. It may be the realization of something deep in your heart. It may be something about God's character that you did not know before. It is as though the Lord takes blinders off of your eyes when this happens. You thought you knew something, but now you *really* know it! This new discovery expresses itself in a new prayer to the Lord. Today, as you begin your time with the Lord, ask God to speak to your heart and to slow you down that you might hear what He says.

READ AND STUDY GOD'S WORD

1. The psalmist knew God's Word well. Therefore, the Lord had a soft and pliable heart to work with, ready to receive what God wanted to show him. The psalmist had so much truth from God that he could think about and reason with and learn from. Look at the following verses from Psalm 119. Record what the psalmist discovered and what he prayed for.

Verse(s) from Psalm 119	What the Psalmist Learned	The Prayer That Followed
19		

Verse(s) from Psalm 119	What the Psalmist Learned	The Prayer That Followed
64		
65-66		
68		
73		
94		
114-116		
125		
156		

2. Which discovery or prayer means the most to you today?

3. Habakkuk was a man of God who was filled with questions for God. He did not understand why there was suffering and why evil people seemed to prosper. Read Habakkuk 3:16-19. What did he discover, and what was his response?

ADORE GOD IN PRAYER

Think about your study this week. What has been the most important truth you have discovered? It might be something in the quotes or verses that you have thought about. Respond to this truth in prayer to the Lord. Record your prayer in your Journal.

YIELD YOURSELF TO GOD

All that true prayer seeks is God Himself, for with Him we get all we need. Prayer is simply "the turning of the soul to God." David describes it as the lifting up of the living soul to the living God. *Unto Thee, O Lord, do I lift up my soul* (Ps. 25:1). What a beautiful description of prayer that is! When we desire the Lord Jesus to behold our souls, we also desire that the beauty of holiness may be upon us. When we lift up our souls to God in prayer it gives God an opportunity to do what He will in us and with us.

AN UNKNOWN CHRISTIAN IN *THE KNEELING CHRISTIAN*

And so we must learn to pray. The child learns to speak because his father speaks to him. He learns the speech of his father. So we learn to speak to God because God has spoken to us and speaks to us. By means of the speech of the Father in heaven his children learn to speak with him. Repeating God's own words after him, we begin to pray to him. . . . God's speech in Jesus Christ meets us in the Holy Scriptures. If we wish to pray with confidence and gladness, then the words of Holy Scripture will have to be the solid basis of our prayer.[1]

DIETRICH BONHOEFFER IN *PSALMS: THE PRAYER BOOK OF THE BIBLE*

ENJOY HIS PRESENCE

O Lord, this morning disperse every mist, and shine clear and strong and invigoratingly. Forgive my tardiness, it takes me so long to awaken to some things. Lord God Omniscient, give me wisdom this day to worship and work aright and be well pleasing to You. Lord, interpret Yourself to me more and more in fullness and beauty. Dark and appalling are the clouds of war and wickedness and we know not where to turn, but Lord God, You reign.[2]

OSWALD CHAMBERS IN *PRAYER: A HOLY OCCUPATION*

REST IN HIS LOVE

"Call to me and I will answer you and tell you great and unsearchable things you do not know" (Jeremiah 33:3, NIV).

bold and influential prayer

Deal bountifully with Your servant,
That I may live and keep Your word.
Open my eyes that I may behold
Wonderful things from Your law.
PSALM 119:17-18

Prepare Your Heart

We live in a desperate hour when thousands are standing at the edge of eternity without choosing to follow Christ. God's words to Ezekiel are timeless: "The people of the land practice extortion and commit robbery; they oppress the poor and needy and mistreat the alien, denying them justice. I looked for a man among them who would build up the wall and stand before me in the gap on behalf of the land so I would not have to destroy it, but I found none" (Ezekiel 22:29-30, NIV).

Daniel was such a man in his time. When he understood from Scripture why his people were in exile and how long it would last, he turned to the Lord in prayer. It was a bold prayer that pleased God. In fact, an angel appeared to Daniel after his prayer and said, "As soon as you began to pray, an answer was given, which I have come to tell you, for you are highly esteemed" (Daniel 9:23, NIV).

Another man who was bold in prayer was Jabez. The history of Jabez and his prayer life are found only in two verses of the Bible. However, the simple truth you learn from Jabez is that God delights in our boldness with Him in prayer, and that kind of prayer can influence thousands.

In the world, many pursue the goal of accumulating as much wealth as possible. In the spiritual realm, if you want to be a person of influence and to participate in God's plan, then you must be a man or woman of prayer. Prayer is what moves God. Before every major revival, there were men and women of God who were moved to extraordinary prayer. Evan Roberts prayed for

203

revival from the age of thirteen and was instrumental in the Welsh Revival. David Brainerd wrestled all night in prayer before seeing revival among the North American Indians in the 1700s.

READ AND STUDY GOD'S WORD

1. Today you will look at how the bold prayers of God's people have influenced their generations. What do you learn about prayer from the lives of these men of God? How did God respond to their prayers?

1 Chronicles 4:9-10 (the prayer of Jabez)

Daniel 9:1-25 (the prayer of Daniel)

2. Which prayer means the most to you today and why?

3. What do you learn from these prayers that you can apply to your own life?

ADORE GOD IN PRAYER

How can you be bold in prayer today? Who are the people on your heart? What circumstances seem impossible—circumstances only God can manage? What do you need today? Turn to your Prayer Pages, and write out your prayers. You might also include Scripture that comes to your mind that you can claim as you pray.

YIELD YOURSELF TO GOD

Believe me, prayer is our highest privilege, our gravest responsibility, and the greatest power God has put into our hands. Prayer, real prayer, is the noblest, the sublimest, the most stupendous act that any creature of God can perform.

AN UNKNOWN CHRISTIAN IN *THE KNEELING CHRISTIAN*

Praying people are God's agents on earth, the representatives of the government of heaven, called to a specific task on the earth. While it is true that the Holy Spirit and the angels are agents of God in carrying forward the redemption of the human race, yet among them there must be praying people. For such people God has great use. He can make much of them, and in the past He has done wonderful things through them. These are God's instruments in carrying out His great purposes on the earth. They are God's messengers, watchmen, shepherds, and workmen, who need not be ashamed. Fully equipped for the great work to which they are appointed, they honor God and bless the world.[1]

E. M. BOUNDS IN *E.M. BOUNDS ON PRAYER*

When we seek God's blessing as the ultimate value in life, we are throwing ourselves entirely into the river of His will and power and purposes for us. All our other needs become secondary to what we really want—which is to become wholly immersed in what God is trying to do in us, through us, and around us for His glory. Let me tell you a guaranteed by-product of sincerely seeking His blessing: Your life will become marked by miracles. How do I know? Because He promises it, and I've seen it happen in my own life! God's power to accomplish great things suddenly finds no obstruction in you. You're moving in His direction. You're praying for exactly what God desires. Suddenly the unhindered forces of heaven can begin to accomplish God's perfect will—through you. And you will be the first to notice![2]

BRUCE WILKINSON IN *THE PRAYER OF JABEZ*

ENJOY HIS PRESENCE
Are you praying on behalf of people and nations? Will you begin today to stand in the gap on behalf of your family, neighbors, church, city, and nation?

REST IN HIS LOVE
"David built there an altar to the LORD and offered burnt offerings and peace offerings. Thus the LORD was moved by prayer for the land, and the plague was held back from Israel" (2 Samuel 24:25).

Dear Friend,

This week you have looked at the prayer of revival. Something happens to your prayers when God revives your heart. Look over your quiet times from this week. What did God do in your prayer life?

How does the change that takes place in your prayers affect your relationship with God?

What were your most meaningful discoveries this week as you spent time with the Lord?
Most meaningful insight:

Most meaningful devotional reading:

Most meaningful verse:

The first hint of revival is frequently a stirring in the life of prayer in the church. However, it is frequently the example of the leaders that brings about this burden for prayer in the church. Hezekiah set the example for the people by his own commitment to God in prayer. When Paul urged Timothy to prayer (I Timothy 2:1), it was in the context of a letter to a Christian leader. . . .

In 1857 revival had come to America and, once again, it was a direct result of prayer. The name of the evangelist Dwight L. Moody is well known, but few are familiar with Jeremiah Lanphier, the New York businessman who became a city missionary. "He had not been a city missionary long before he sent out an advertisement for a noon-day prayer meeting to be held on Wednesdays in the Dutch Church at the corner of Fulton Street in downtown New York. This man went to the room that he had hired. Five, ten, fifteen, twenty, twenty-five minutes went by, and no one turned up, until after he had waited half an hour, six others came one after the other. They prayed, and the next week there were twenty, and the famous Fulton Street prayer meeting had begun. The first week in October it was decided to hold the meeting daily instead of weekly, and within six months 10,000 businessmen were meeting every day to pray for revival. Within two years a million converts had been added to the American churches."[1]

BRIAN H. EDWARDS IN *REVIVAL: A PEOPLE SATURATED WITH GOD*

the power in revival

week
eight

PSALM 119:170

only God can do the work

Let my supplication come before You;
Deliver me according to Your word.
PSALM 119:170

Prepare Your Heart

There is a time in believers' lives when they realize that nothing in themselves can enable them to change, handle a circumstance, understand God's perspective, or have hope in the midst of a difficulty. They can only cast themselves onto the mercy of God and rely on Him for the work. That is the place to be in order to experience the power of revival—for the power in revival is in God Himself. The triune God is at work: God the Father, God the Son, and God the Holy Spirit. God does something only He can do.

Andrew Murray, a quiet and deeply effective man of God, discovered this secret after serving for ten years as a minister. Early in his life with the Lord, he was earnest and zealous. Yet his heart burned with dissatisfaction. He felt he had no power for service. Then one day a friend shared with him that if God placed a desire in his heart, God would fulfill it. That statement was profound to him, and he thought about it over and over. In the next few years, the Lord gave Murray a new eternal perspective. Here is how he describes the change: "I have learnt to place myself before God every day, as a vessel to be filled with His Holy Spirit. He has filled me with the blessed assurance that He, as the everlasting God, has guaranteed His work in me. If there is one lesson that I am learning day by day, it is this: that it is God who worketh all in all. Oh that I could help any brother or sister to realize this."[1]

Paul came to this same realization: *not I but Christ.* Only one life is at work within: the life of Jesus Christ. His power. His strength. His comfort. His joy. His peace. His love. His wisdom. His holiness. His humility. His overcoming nature. As you are personally revived, you discover that you have within you the Resource beyond all resources to meet every need: Christ Himself. You can say with Paul, "I have been crucified with Christ; and it is no longer I who live, but Christ lives in me; and the life which I now live in the flesh I live by faith in the

Son of God, who loved me and gave Himself up for me" (Galatians 2:20). When Christ is your life, others will notice and be drawn to you, not because you are so great, but because they see His beauty, His love, His holiness. He is the One who will reach out through you and touch their lives.

READ AND STUDY GOD'S WORD

1. The triune God is at work in you "to will and to work for His good pleasure" (Philippians 2:13). Jesus explained this work of God to His disciples. Turn to John 14. Read this chapter slowly, verse by verse, and record everything you learn about the Father, Jesus Christ, the Holy Spirit (the Helper, or Counselor), those who believe in Jesus, and the world.

God the Father

Jesus Christ

the Holy Spirit (the Helper)

those who believe in Jesus

the world

2. What are the most significant promises to the believer in John 14?

3. Which promise means the most to you today? Why is it significant to you?

ADORE GOD IN PRAYER

What areas of your life need the Lord's work today? What burdens are you carrying? Use one of your Prayer Pages to list those areas. Ask the Lord to be the strength and the answer in every need. Roll those burdens onto the triune God, who makes His home in you.

YIELD YOURSELF TO GOD

O my soul! Yield yourself to the mighty influence of this word: *Of God you are in Christ Jesus.* It is the same God of whom Christ is made all that He is for us, of whom we also are in Christ, and will most surely be made what we must be to Him. Take time to meditate and to worship, until the light that comes from the throne of God has shone into you, and you have seen your union to Christ as indeed the work of His almighty Father. Take time, day after day, and let, in your whole religious life, with all it has of claims and duties, of needs and wishes, God be everything. See Jesus, as He speaks to you, *Abide in Me,* pointing upward and saying, *My Father is the husbandman. Of Him you are in Me, through Him you abide in Me, and to Him and to His glory shall be the fruit you bear.* And let your answer be, Amen, Lord! So be it. From eternity Christ and I were ordained for each other; inseparably we belong to each other: it is God's will; I shall abide in Christ. It is of God I am in Christ Jesus.

ANDREW MURRAY IN *ABIDE IN CHRIST*

ENJOY HIS PRESENCE

Think about what it means that Christ is your life. How does that make a difference in your circumstances? How will His strength, comfort, love, and peace make a difference in you today? The power in revival is manifest in your life in this way: "Christ in you, the hope of glory" (Colossians 1:27).

REST IN HIS LOVE

"For you died, and your life is now hidden with Christ in God. When Christ, who is your life, appears, then you also will appear with him in glory" (Colossians 3:3-4, NIV).

He teaches me

I have not turned aside from Your ordinances,
For You Yourself have taught me.
PSALM 119:102

Prepare Your Heart

How is it possible to understand the things of God and to gain God's perspective in any situation? The psalmist understood that God was his Teacher. The power in revival is God. Part of restoring you to His purposes is teaching you His ways. You can have human teachers who teach you about God's Word, but there is only one real Teacher. Jesus promised that "the Counselor, the Holy Spirit, whom the Father will send in my name, will teach you all things and will remind you of everything I have said to you" (John 14:26, NIV).

Do you desire to learn from the Lord? The Teacher lives in you. When you sit down with God's Word, you are never alone. God is always there, ready to meet you on the pages of Scripture, ready to show you His character and ways. Ask Him today to teach you those things that are on His heart to show you.

READ AND STUDY GOD'S WORD

1. The psalmist did not go to earthly teachers to learn about God. He asked God to teach him. Look at the following verses and record what the psalmist learned from God:

verse 26

verse 66

verse 98

verse 105

verse 125

verse 130

2. One of the things that Jesus did while on earth was teach. Imagine what it must have been like to sit at His feet. Record your observations about the teaching ministry of Jesus. Include the responses of those who listened to Him.

Mark 11:17-18

Luke 11:1-13

John 7:14-16

John 8:2

3. The Lord is your Teacher even now through the Holy Spirit. From the following
verses, record what you learn about His teaching ministry and what He teaches you.
  John 14:26

  John 16:12-15

  Romans 8:16

  1 Corinthians 2:6-13

  Colossians 2:1-3

  2 Timothy 2:7

  James 1:5

  James 3:17

  1 John 3:24

  1 John 5:20

4. Summarize what the Lord teaches His children as they study His Word.

ADORE GOD IN PRAYER
Talk with the Lord about what He has taught you today. Ask Him to give you ears to hear and eyes to see His truth.

YIELD YOURSELF TO GOD
The Father sends the Holy Spirit to lead you into all truth. Jesus said that "when He, the Spirit of truth, comes, He will guide you into all the truth; for He will not speak on His own initiative, but whatever He hears, He will speak; and He will disclose to you what is to come. He will glorify Me, for He will take of Mine and will disclose it to you" (John 16:13-14). F. B. Meyer points out in *Gospel of John*:

> The Spirit's presence, as such, should not be a subject of our close scrutiny, lest we conflict with his holy purpose of being hidden, that Jesus may be all in all before the gaze of saint and sinner. He is so anxious that nothing should divert the soul's gaze from the Lord whom He would reveal, that He carefully withdraws Himself from view. . . . But remember that when you have the most precious views of your dear Lord, it is because the Holy Spirit, all unseen, is witnessing and working within you.[1]

ENJOY HIS PRESENCE
What has God been teaching you lately? What is the most important truth He has taught you in the last month?

REST IN HIS LOVE
"It is because of him that you are in Christ Jesus, who has become for us wisdom from God — that is, our righteousness, holiness and redemption" (1 Corinthians 1:30, NIV).

He comforts me

O may Your lovingkindness comfort me,
According to Your word to Your servant.
PSALM 119:76

Prepare Your Heart

How do saints like Corrie ten Boom, Darlene Rose, Martin Luther, the apostle Paul, and so many others endure such traumatic hardships? When their faith is on trial, how can they make it through? They have the Holy Spirit within, who is their Helper, their Comforter. So do you.

There is nothing like the comfort of the Lord. Friends may offer comforting words. But when the Lord applies His comfort to your heart, it has the power to heal you and calm your pain. You don't necessarily escape your circumstance. However, His comfort carries you through the ordeal. No human can do this.

Begin your time today by meditating on Psalm 23. You might even choose to look at it in several different translations. This is a familiar psalm, but is one of great comfort to all saints in need. What does it mean to you today? You might write a prayer to the Lord using those words that stand out to you in this psalm.

READ AND STUDY GOD'S WORD

1. The psalmist in Psalm 119 drew near to God time and again for comfort. As you read the following verses, write out the different truths about God that comforted him. These

same truths can bring comfort today to you.
  verses 49-50

  verse 58

  verse 65

  verse 76

  verse 77

  verse 90

  verse 94

  verse 114

  verse 116

  verse 117

  verse 132

  verse 151

  verse 153

2. As you look at these verses and think about the comfort of the Lord in the psalmist's life, what is your favorite truth that can carry you through the most difficult times?

3. How does God comfort you in a time of trouble? Record what you see in the following verses.

Acts 9:31

2 Corinthians 1:1-7

2 Thessalonians 2:16-17

ADORE GOD IN PRAYER

> Lord God Almighty,
> I ask not to be enrolled amongst the earthly great and rich,
> but to be numbered with the spiritually blessed.
> Make it my present, supreme, persevering concern
> to obtain those blessings which are
> spiritual in their nature,
> eternal in their continuance,
> satisfying in their possession.
> Preserve me from a false estimate of the whole or a part of my character;
> May I pay regard to my principles as well as my conduct,
> my motives as well as my actions.
> Help me never to mistake the excitement of my passions
> for the renewing of the Holy Spirit,
> never to judge my religion by occasional impressions and impulses, but by my constant and prevailing disposition.
> May my heart be right with thee, and my life as becometh the gospel.
> May I maintain a supreme regard to another and better world,
> and feel and confess myself a stranger and a pilgrim here.
> Afford me all the direction, defence, support, and consolation
> my journey hence requires,

and grant me a mind stayed upon thee.
Give me large abundance of the supply of the Spirit of Jesus,
that I may be prepared for every duty,
love thee in all my mercies,
submit to thee in every trial,
trust thee when walking in darkness,
have peace amidst life's changes.
Lord, I believe, help thou my unbelief and uncertainties.[1]

FROM *THE VALLEY OF VISION*

YIELD YOURSELF TO GOD

If we look to the present state of the church of Christ, it is as Daniel in the midst of lions, as a lily amongst thorns, as a ship not only tossed but almost covered with waves. It is so low that the enemies think they have buried Christ, with respect to his gospel, in the grave, and there they think to keep him from rising. But as Christ rose in his person, so he will roll away all stones and rise again in his church. How little support has the church and cause of Christ at this day! How strong a conspiracy is against it! The spirit of antichrist is now lifted up and marches furiously. Things seem to hang on a small and invisible thread. But our comfort is that Christ lives and reigns, and stands on Mount Zion in defence of those who stand for him (Revelation 14:1); and when states and kingdoms shall dash one against another Christ will have care of his own children and cause, seeing there is nothing else in the world that he much esteems. At this very time the delivery of his church and the ruin of his enemies are in progress. We see nothing in motion till Christ has done his work, and then we shall see that the Lord reigns. Christ and his church, when they are at the lowest, are nearest rising. His enemies, at the highest, are nearest their downfall.[2]

RICHARD SIBBES IN *THE BRUISED REED*

ENJOY HIS PRESENCE
How has the Lord comforted you in trials? Thank Him today for meeting you in these difficulties. Close by meditating on the words of this hymn by Civilla D. Martin:

Be not dismayed whate'er betide, God will take care of you;
beneath his wings of love abide, God will take care of you.

Refrain: God will take care of you, through every day, o'er all the way;
he will take care of you, God will take care of you.

REST IN HIS LOVE
"A bruised reed he will not break, and a smoldering wick he will not snuff out" (Isaiah 42:3, NIV).

He strengthens me

My soul weeps because of grief;
Strengthen me according to Your word.
PSALM 119:28

Prepare Your Heart

Every believer has certain things or people that seem to drag him or her down. They are the "if-onlys" of life. "If only my spouse were a strong Christian. If only I didn't have this weakness or fear. If only I had more free time. If only I didn't have this job. If only I hadn't become ill. If only I could have all the good things my neighbor has. If only I had more money." Sometimes these things might appear to be liabilities. Alan Redpath calls them "the ministry of the thorn."[1]

Today you will see why weakness is a good thing in the Christian's life. So many things in the eternal perspective are paradoxes. When you are weak, you are strong. The way down is the way up. It is imperative that you live in God's Word so you might learn the language of heaven.

READ AND STUDY GOD'S WORD

1. Turn to 2 Corinthians 12:1-10. What did Paul experience? What did he learn from it?

2. What can you learn from Paul that will help you in your own life?

3. Why can you be strong in weakness? What are the advantages of weakness in a believer's life? Record your insights as you read the following verses.
 Romans 8:35-39

 2 Corinthians 4:7-12

 Ephesians 6:10

 2 Timothy 1:7

 1 Peter 4:11

4. Why do you think power is perfected in weakness? Why is it that when you are weak you are strong? Keep in mind all that you have learned from Paul's life.

ADORE GOD IN PRAYER

In what areas of your life are you weak? Take each of these areas to the Lord today and ask Him to be your strength. Then, begin to watch for His work in your life. He will show Himself to be strong in you.

YIELD YOURSELF TO GOD

Surely the sufferings and limitations of this present time will not be worthy to be compared with the exceeding weight of glory, when in the presence of our Lord we shall see eye to eye, and know even as we are known. In the light of these words we may get comfort. When some crushing trouble befalls us, He who only spoke as they were able to bear will not permit the flame to be hotter, the tide stronger, or the task more trying, than we have strength for. We often do not know our strength nor the power of His grace. Sorrow may be sent to reveal us to ourselves, and show how much spiritual energy we have been silently acquiring. Do not therefore run to and fro and say, "it is too much, I cannot bear it." But know and be sure that Christ has ascertained your resources, and is sure of your ability, before He permits the extreme ordeal to overtake you. Dare to say with the Apostle, *I can do all things through Christ who strengtheneth me.*[2]

F. B. MEYER IN *GOSPEL OF JOHN*

The Lord Jesus watches because He allows the pressure to continue in order that, in the severest moment of testing, it may drive you to His wounded side, and teach you that for overwhelming pressure there is adequate grace. Oh, would it not be wonderful if that experience could be yours today! Stop praying for the removal of the thorn, and understand the transforming power of the cross![3]

ALAN REDPATH IN *BLESSINGS OUT OF BUFFETINGS*

ENJOY HIS PRESENCE
Close your time by meditating on the words of this hymn by Elisha A. Hoffman.

What a fellowship, what a joy divine, leaning on the everlasting arms;
what a blessedness, what a peace is mine, leaning on the everlasting arms.

Refrain:
Leaning, leaning, safe and secure from all alarms;
leaning, leaning, leaning on the everlasting arms.

O how sweet to walk in this pilgrim way, leaning on the everlasting arms;
O how bright the path grows from day to day, leaning on the everlasting arms.

Refrain

What have I to dread, what have I to fear, leaning on the everlasting arms?
I have blessed peace with my Lord so near, leaning on the everlasting arms.

Refrain

Rest in His Love

"And what more shall I say? I do not have time to tell about Gideon, Barak, Samson, Jephthah, David, Samuel and the prophets, who through faith conquered kingdoms, administered justice, and gained what was promised; who shut the mouths of lions, quenched the fury of the flames, and escaped the edge of the sword; whose weakness was turned to strength; and who became powerful in battle and routed foreign armies" (Hebrews 11:32-34, NIV).

He changes me

I shall run the way of Your commandments,
For You will enlarge my heart.
PSALM 119:32

Prepare Your Heart

A woman was about to lose her life because she had been caught in adultery. The religious leaders brought her to Jesus. They reminded Him that the Law of Moses demanded that she be stoned. Then they asked Him what He had to say about it. He told them that if they were sinless, then they could punish her for this sin. None of them could do it. In fact, the oldest ones in the group left first. They had lived long enough to know they could never change themselves and they were not perfect. It took the younger ones a little longer to leave.

The woman was left alone with Jesus. He looked into her eyes and told her that He did not condemn her and that she should go and leave her life of sin. Somehow, He gave her the hope of a changed life, a new lifestyle that was not like the adulterous one that she had become trapped in (see John 8:1-11).

Saul experienced a similar radical change. He was a sharp Jewish Bible student and an innovative leader. He was outraged that another group of Jews claimed that Jesus, who had been executed as a criminal, was the Messiah. So Saul invested all his energy in having these followers of Jesus arrested and, in some cases, executed. Then one day, on the road to Damascus, a blinding light flashed all around Saul. He heard a voice like no other that he had ever heard. It commanded and questioned him with authority.

The voice asked, "Saul, Saul, why do you persecute me?" He replied, "Who are you, Lord?" The voice answered, "I am Jesus, whom you are persecuting. . . . Now get up and go into the city, and you will be told what you must do" (Acts 9:4-6, NIV). Blinded, Saul had to be led by the hand into Damascus. This moment of humiliation and brokenness led to new

227

life. Saul was given back his sight and also enabled to see the truth of Jesus, that He was indeed the Messiah. Immediately, Saul was filled with the desire to preach in the synagogues about Jesus. This was not an impulse or passion that was humanly manufactured. The Jews were baffled by the power with which he spoke and by the message that he gave. The change in Saul ultimately influenced the entire world. Because of Jesus, he became Paul, the apostle to the Gentiles.

The gospel of Jesus Christ offers the promise of new life, filled with meaning and purpose. This new life is possible because we become new creations, transformed by Jesus Christ through His life within us. This is what personal revival is all about. God changes you from within and carries out His purposes in your life.

Turn to John 8:1-11 and think about this event as a preparation of heart for your time with the Lord today.

READ AND STUDY GOD'S WORD

1. The author of Psalm 119 experienced the transforming power of God in his life. According to the following verses, in what ways did God transform him?
   verse 32

   verse 133

2. In what areas of your life do you need your heart to be enlarged (NASB), "set . . . free" (NIV), or "helped" (NLT) so that you might obey God's Word (verse 32)?

3. It is very important to understand how the Holy Spirit transforms you. According to Ephesians 1:14, the Father gives you the Holy Spirit as a pledge, or deposit, that guarantees your eternal inheritance. According to these verses, how does the Holy Spirit work in your life to transform you?
   John 16:7-15

   Acts 1:8

Romans 8:6

Romans 12:1-2

2 Corinthians 3:17-18

Galatians 5:22-23

Ephesians 5:18 ("filled" means controlled and empowered)

1 Peter 1:2

ADORE GOD IN PRAYER

In what ways have you seen the Lord change your life? Thank Him for His work in your life today.

YIELD YOURSELF TO GOD

Be filled with the Spirit. Notice two or three things about that. First of all, observe that the verb is *passive—Be filled.* It is nothing you have to do; it is rather something you have to let God do. God comes and He bids us let Him have His own way with us in growth and development, even as He had His way with us in the new birth. You were born again when you received Jesus Christ. When you received Jesus Christ you received God; and when God received you, you received the Spirit of God. If you are Christ's, you have the Holy Spirit. But there is a difference between having the Holy Spirit and being filled with the Spirit. It is a difference, not of kind, but of degree; and the reason for our stunted development is that we have not been willing to let God come into our lives and do in us that which we could never do for ourselves. Some of us have been striving for such a blessing as this. We have been struggling and wrestling to attain it. We have been full of good resolutions and good desires, and we have striven and struggled to bring these resolves to the birth. But nine times out of ten we have failed, and all the time God has been saying to us, *Be still and know that I am God*.

Then it is not only passive, but the verb is imperative—*be filled with the Spirit*. It is a command. It leaves you and me no option in the matter. It is just as much God's command as any other command. God does not propose that there should be two classes of believers—those who are Spirit-filled and those who are not Spirit-filled. The fact of the command being given shows only too clearly that there is a need for it. So many of us have but little of God in our lives, and so little of that practical setting forth of God's beauty in life and conduct, and so little real desire to be pleasing to Him. Therefore, we are to be filled.

Also notice that the verse is in the present tense, and the present tense in the grammar of the New Testament always implies something which has a definite beginning, and leads on to a course of events and of experience and of happening. You are to be filled with the Spirit this morning. But the blessing of this morning will not do for the needs of tomorrow. The blessing of today will not suffice for next week; and it is your privilege, dear child of God, to keep on being filled with the Spirit, God continually pouring of His fullness into your heart, and you continually receiving it, and continually, by His grace, transmuting that fullness into the expression of life and character and personality.[1]

REV. J. RUSSELL HOWDEN (B. D.) IN *KESWICK'S AUTHENTIC VOICE*

ENJOY HIS PRESENCE

How can you be filled with the Spirit today? First, confess any sins that the Lord shows you. Then simply ask the Lord to fill you with His Holy Spirit. According to 1 John 5:14-15, "if we ask anything according to his will, he hears us. And if we know that he hears us—whatever we ask—we know that we have what we asked of him" (NIV). Therefore, because being filled with God's Spirit is His desire for you, you can know that He answers your prayer. Walk in His transforming power and strength today and watch what His work of revival does in your life and in the lives around you.

REST IN HIS LOVE

"The mind of sinful man is death, but the mind controlled by the Spirit is life and peace" (Romans 8:6, NIV).

DEAR FRIEND,

In your quiet times this week you have looked at the ministry of the Holy Spirit in your personal spiritual revival. After all that you have seen in God's Word, why is the Holy Spirit important in your life?

You have also seen this week that the triune God is the power in revival—He is the One who works in you to make you the person He wants you to be. In what ways does God work in your life?

What were your most meaningful discoveries this week as you spent time with the Lord?

Most meaningful insight:

Most meaningful devotional reading:

Most meaningful verse:

As you close your quiet times this week, think about these challenging words of Robert Coleman from his book *The Coming World Revival*:

Every member of the congregation should look upon revival as a personal responsibility and find the place of service most suited to his or her talents and personality. The time has come to quit ascribing the problem to other people in the church. What about you? Regardless of your position in the church and whatever gifts you may possess, have you fulfilled the conditions for revival in your own life? Are you completely open to the Spirit's direction? Is your heart cleansed from every evil desire and selfish purpose? Mere concern for revival is not enough. Is your heart, your home, your business a witness to the overflowing love of God?[1]

the life and purpose of revival

week
nine

PSALM 119:116

blessing

How blessed are those whose way is blameless,
Who walk in the law of the LORD.
PSALM 119:1

Prepare Your Heart

There is something that is etched all across the pages of Scripture, from the first chapter of Genesis to the last chapter of Revelation. There is something that separates those who know Jesus Christ from those who don't. It is the plan and purpose of God.

The Christian life has been compared to a race in which we are all runners. God desires that we not simply finish but that we win the prize. God desires that we go for the gold. The intangible quality that separates participants from winners is the will to win and an even greater desire not to lose. Those who go for the gold will set aside anything that might hinder them from winning. When you stand face to face with your Lord and you hear those words, "Well done, good and faithful servant," then you will know it was worth going for the gold.

There is a purpose in all of life for the one who walks with the Lord. Nothing is wasted if you know Him. No trial. No circumstance. No suffering. God is always causing everything to "work together for good to those . . . who are called according to His purpose" (Romans 8:28). Those who do not know Christ cannot have that same experience, for they are not becoming who God wants them to be nor participating in God's plan. Personal revival has been defined as a quickening of heart and soul by God, imparting whatever is necessary to sustain one's spiritual life and enable a return to the experience of one's true purpose as ordained by God. In order for you to understand personal revival, it is imperative that you know what your true purpose is in life.

What is life all about? Is it about movies, possessions, jobs, church, ministry, people, or money? Of course, life in this world is filled with such things. But is that really life? Jesus made an incredible claim in John 10:10: "I came that they may have life, and have it abundantly." When Jesus spoke of abundant life, He was promising something more than we could ever use up in a lifetime. He was promising something full and meaningful. Personal revival is life as it is meant to be.

We have seen that God promises personal revival and has a pattern for how He does it. His plan involves His invitation to an intimate relationship and our response of humility, our pursuit of God, and our obedience to what He says in His Word. When we respond like this, He restores us to His purposes. Our example of revival has been the author of Psalm 119. His heart was troubled because of the trials of his life, so he prayed, "Revive me, O LORD." God revived his heart through His Word in the power of the Holy Spirit.

The pattern of personal revival also involves death to self, brokenness, and surrender to God. This is part of the process of becoming who God wants us to be. The pattern involves prayer; that is why Psalm 119 is a prayer. And the one who does the work in revival is God Himself.

Now, what is the result of a life of personal spiritual revival? It is the abundant life that Jesus promised. Life as it is meant to be. Everyone wants abundant life, but few know that the way to it is by knowing God and being daily revived by Him.

Today, as you begin your quiet time, turn to Psalm 139:1-16. Think about what these words mean for you. Read through the words as though you are saying them to the Lord about yourself. Then write a prayer to the Lord in your Journal, thanking Him for the privilege of personal revival. Ask Him to "open [your] eyes that [you] may behold wonderful things from [His] law" (Psalm 119:18).

READ AND STUDY GOD'S WORD

One of the great words in the Bible is *blessed*. This word in the Hebrew is *esher*. It occurs forty-four times in the Old Testament. Blessing is the enjoyment that comes not from circumstances but from the favor of God. The New Testament word is *makarios*, which includes the satisfaction and fulfillment that comes from Christ, who indwells each believer.

Blessing is independent of circumstances. The happiness of the world is entirely dependent on feelings and circumstances. That is why personal revival is revolutionary. It is life on the highest plane. You can experience the abundant life no matter where you are and no matter what is happening. You experience God's favor through the presence of Christ, so you have deep satisfaction within.

1. The psalmist knew about God's blessing. Look at these verses in Psalm 119 and record who is blessed.

verse 1

verse 2

verse 12

2. God has had this promise of blessing in mind for you from the very beginning. What do you learn about God's blessing from the following events? Note who will be blessed and what is the promised blessing. If you are short on time, choose just one or two of these passages. (If you need more space, use your Journal.)

Passage of Scripture	Who Will Be Blessed	Promised Blessing
Genesis 1:27-28; 5:2		
Genesis 12:1-3		
Genesis 22:15-18		
Deuteronomy 11:8-15,26-28		
Jeremiah 17:7-8		
Matthew 5:1-11		
Matthew 25:31-36		
Revelation 22:14		

3. *Optional:* What kinds of things bring about God's blessing?
   Luke 11:28

   Luke 12:42-43

Ephesians 1:3-8

James 1:12-14

1 Peter 4:13

4. Why would someone want to experience God's blessing? What does God's blessing mean to you today?

ADORE GOD IN PRAYER
Today is a day to thank the Lord for how He has blessed you. In your Journal, list all the ways God has brought His blessing into your life. Thank Him for each blessing.

YIELD YOURSELF TO GOD

All Christians have what the New Testament calls *eternal life*, for without this one cannot be a Christian; but not all Christians have entered into the experience of abounding life. There can be relationship without fellowship; there can be union without communion; there can be life without health; there can be privilege without enjoyment; there can be movement without progress. One may war and yet not win, may serve and yet not succeed, may try and yet not triumph; and the difference throughout is just the difference between the possession of eternal life, and the experience of abounding life; the difference between *peace with God* and *the peace of God*; the difference between obtainment and attainment. Abounding life is just the fullness of life in Christ, made possible by His death and resurrection, and made actual by the indwelling and infilling of the Holy Spirit. It is not the will of God that we should be as fruitless trees, as waterless clouds, or as savourless salt; but that we should fulfill the highest functions of our Christian calling. Christ's promise is that He will satisfy the thirst of all who come to Him, and His purpose for those who come is that *from their innermost being shall flow rivers of living water.*[1]

REV. W. GRAHAM SCROGGIE (D. D.) IN *KESWICK'S AUTHENTIC VOICE*

ENJOY HIS PRESENCE

How have God's blessings in your life spilled over into the lives of those around you? That is what happens in personal spiritual revival. As you are revived, there is an effect in others' lives. Are you experiencing the abundant life that the Lord promises? What have you learned in this study that helps you to know His abundant life?

REST IN HIS LOVE

"Praise be to the God and Father of our Lord Jesus Christ, who has blessed us in the heavenly realms with every spiritual blessing in Christ" (Ephesians 1:3, NIV).

joy

I have rejoiced in the way of Your testimonies,
As much as in all riches.
PSALM 119:14

Prepare Your Heart

There is no mistaking one who has gone deep with God. The quality that stands out in such a person is joy. Joy comes from the presence of God. It is the delight in the heart that comes from knowing God's character and ways. We have the privilege to be in a relationship with the God of the universe, who loves us. Joy depends on God, while happiness depends on circumstances. Joy is not irrational, nor does it necessarily produce exuberant emotion, but it is steadfast and vibrant like a constantly moving stream of water. True joy is contagious.

Today, as a preparation of heart, meditate on Psalm 33. Record any verses that are significant to you.

READ AND STUDY GOD'S WORD

1. When God spoke in the Old Testament of the life He wanted for His people, joy was one quality He talked about. Read Deuteronomy 12:1-18. What does God say there about joy?

2. In John 15:9-11, what do you see about joy?

In his commentary on John, Leon Morris points out that this joy is the result of a fruitful life.[1] It is the same kind of joy that an artist feels in something new he or she has created. Morris says the Lord is implying that we share in His joy over the work He produces. Is there anything so exciting as seeing a life changed for Jesus Christ? To be a part of what God is doing in the world, to actually be able to participate with Him as He changes lives, is the cause of great joy.

3. What do you learn about joy from the following verses? Personalize your answers.
   Nehemiah 8:10

   Luke 15:8-10

   John 16:22

   Acts 13:49-52

   Galatians 5:22

   Hebrews 12:1-2

   1 Peter 1:8

   Jude 24

4. What does the joy of the Lord mean to you today? How has His joy been your strength? In what ways do you need His joy today? Record your insights.

Adore God in Prayer
You had the opportunity to meditate on Psalm 33 earlier in your quiet time today. Take those words and personalize them into a prayer to the Lord.

Yield Yourself to God

Gladness! I like to cultivate the spirit of gladness! It puts the soul so in tune again, and keeps it in tune, so that Satan is shy of touching it!—the chords of the soul become too warm, or too full of heavenly electricity, for his infernal fingers, and he goes off somewhere else! Satan is always very shy of meddling with me when my heart is full of gladness and joy in the Holy Ghost.[2]

MRS. CHARLES COWMAN IN *STREAMS IN THE DESERT*

Enjoy His Presence
What is it that brings you joy in life? Do you know the joy of the Lord? What difference do you think the joy of the Lord makes in the lives of those around you?

Rest in His Love
"To him who is able to keep you from falling and to present you before his glorious presence without fault and with great joy—to the only God our Savior be glory, majesty, power and authority, through Jesus Christ our Lord, before all ages, now and forevermore! Amen" (Jude 24, NIV).

fruitfulness

I will also speak of Your testimonies before kings
And shall not be ashamed.
PSALM 119:46

Prepare Your Heart

B ill Bright, a firm agnostic at the time, left Oklahoma for Southern California to seek his fortune in business. On his first evening in Los Angeles, he picked up a hitchhiker who was the roommate of Dawson Trotman, founder of The Navigators. Bill spent his first night in California visiting the homes of Trotman and Charles E. Fuller, the founder of the radio program *Old Fashioned Revival Hour*. Bright began attending Hollywood's First Presbyterian Church, and largely through that church's influence and his mother's prayers, he became a Christian in 1945. At First Presbyterian, he met Dr. Henrietta Mears, who began to give him a vision for the world and its need for Jesus Christ. Mears said, "There is no magic in small plans. When I consider my ministry, I think of the world. Anything less than that would not be worthy of Christ nor of His will for my life."

While Bright's business prospered, his commitment to Jesus Christ grew. He attended Fuller Theological Seminary and in 1948 married Vonette Zachary. In 1951, the couple signed a covenant together in which they renounced every material ambition. While studying for a Greek exam one night, Bright was overwhelmed with the Lord's presence and the command to help fulfill the Great Commission by taking the gospel throughout the world. He felt he was to begin this calling by taking the gospel to college students. Thus began Campus Crusade for Christ.

In the first year, Campus Crusade saw at least 250 students make decisions to receive Christ as their personal Savior. Now, more than fifty years later, there are tens of thousands of staff members in every corner of the world. As a result of Campus Crusade for Christ, and the millions of Christians they have helped train, the gospel has been taken to more than one billion people. Campus Crusade's goal is "to help give every man, woman, and child in the entire world an opportunity to find new life in Jesus Christ."[1]

Where did Dr. Bill Bright get such a lofty goal? In the opening pages of one of CCC's campus ministry manuals is this explanation:

> The need of the hour is for Christians to recapture the vision and strategy contained in our Lord's command to eleven men, *Go ye into all the world and make disciples of all nations.* This was the Lord's Great Commission and obviously a challenge that the disciples could not fulfill. However, the Holy Spirit of God was able to move through those few channels and reproduce reproducers so rapidly that the known world heard the claims of Christ in the first century. The gospel penetrated lives with such power that a pagan Roman Empire was "turned upside down."[2]

Psalm 119 shows how God wants to work through you to touch the world around you. He revives you in order to make you a testimony to His people and to the world. As God revives you, you will be increasingly burdened with the needs of others. You will begin to think of ways to reach out to those around you. You will see ways that you can demonstrate love to your family. God will open your eyes to areas of service in your church. And some-times God will give you a big idea—an idea for a ministry that may reach hundreds of thou-sands of people around the world. None of this is by accident. It is a direct result of God personally reviving you.

In Acts 1:8 Jesus promised His disciples that "you will receive power when the Holy Spirit has come upon you; and you shall be My witnesses in Jerusalem, and in all Judea and Samaria, and even to the remotest part of the earth." Part of the abundant life of personal revival is a fruitfulness that draws others to salvation and nourishes believers. Fruitfulness is one of God's great purposes for you. Every day is a new day filled with opportunity to share your faith, disciple others, share the love of Christ, and grow in His grace. Life never gets boring. It is a great adventure. You can never say, "Is that all there is?"

If you read the biographies of men and women who loved God, such as Jim Elliot, Amy Carmichael, Charles Spurgeon, Oswald Chambers, A. W. Tozer, D. L. Moody, and C. T. Studd, you will notice that the outcome of their lives was fruitfulness. Others were drawn to a deeper love of Christ and a deeper fellowship with each other. The gospel spreads among those who are perishing.

Ministry may be defined as "Jesus Christ in action." He ministers in and through us. God can do amazing things through those who will give themselves to His purposes. It has been said that the world has yet to see what God can do in and through the lives of those who are wholly yielded to Him.

Today, draw near to the Lord and ask Him to quiet your heart. How is your passion for the lost these days? Are you living for the Lord? Have you given yourself to His purposes? Write a prayer in your Journal, expressing all that is on your heart.

READ AND STUDY GOD'S WORD

1. When someone asked Peter just before the Crucifixion about his friendship with Jesus, he failed miserably. He denied even knowing Jesus. That was before Pentecost and the filling of the Holy Spirit. Read Acts 2 and note the difference in Peter. What did the Lord do through the power of the Holy Spirit?

2. What do you learn from the following verses about what God desires to do in and through you?

2 Corinthians 2:14-17

2 Corinthians 5:20

Colossians 1:10-11

2 Timothy 2:2

3. How does fruitfulness contribute to the kind of life Jesus promises to those who are personally revived?

ADORE GOD IN PRAYER

Use the following words by Charles Wesley as a prayer to the Lord:

Give me the faith which can remove and sink the mountain to a plain;
give me the childlike praying love, which longs to build thy house again;
thy love, let it my heart o'er-power, and all my simple soul devour.

I would the precious time redeem, and longer live for this alone,
to spend and to be spent for them who have not yet my Savior known;
fully on these my mission prove, and only breathe, to breathe thy love.

My talents, gifts, and graces, Lord, into thy blessed hands receive;
and let me live to preach thy word, and let me to thy glory live;
my every sacred moment spent in publishing the sinner's Friend.

Enlarge, inflame, and fill my heart with boundless charity divine,
so shall I all my strength exert, and love them with a zeal like thine,
and lead them to thy open side, the sheep for whom the Shepherd died.

Yield Yourself to God

Revival leaders are men with hearts on fire. It is as if God has invaded their lives in every part and taken them captive; they are men who love God, trust in him, hold fast to him and never cease to follow him. Their ministry is not a job, still less an interest or hobby; rather it is an all-consuming passion. And they fear above everything losing the sense of the presence of God. Most of the great men of revival had a strong hold on theology, but never at the expense of a vivid and life-changing relationship with God.[3]

BRIAN EDWARDS IN *REVIVAL: A PEOPLE SATURATED WITH GOD*

Enjoy His Presence

God longs to include you in His plans to reach a lost, hurting world. Have you answered His call to "go therefore and make disciples of all the nations, baptizing them in the name of the Father and the Son and the Holy Spirit, teaching them to observe all that [Jesus] commanded you" (Matthew 28:19-20)? When people hear your words and look at your actions, do they know you love the Lord with all your heart? Are you consumed with the purposes of Christ, or with the empty things of this world? How much do you long to hear God say, "Well done, good and faithful servant"?

Resolve today that you will answer His call and say "Yes, Lord" to whatever and wherever He calls you. The Lord will place ideas for ministry on your heart. Begin to pray about these things. Ask the Lord what He would have you do. And look for opportunities in the areas of ministry that are on your heart.

Rest in His Love

"For the eyes of the LORD range throughout the earth to strengthen those whose hearts are fully committed to him" (2 Chronicles 16:9, NIV).

glory

Make Your face shine upon Your servant,
And teach me Your statutes.
PSALM 119:135

Prepare Your Heart

In the Old Testament we catch glimpses of the kind of relationship we may enjoy with our Lord. One unique relationship was between Moses and God: "The LORD would speak to Moses face to face, as a man speaks with his friend" (Exodus 33:11, NIV). This is the kind of intimacy we may enjoy with our Lord.

The Williams New Testament version of Jesus' words in John 14:23 says, "If anyone really loves me, he will observe my teaching, and my Father will love him, and both of us will come in face-to-face fellowship with him; yes, we will make our special dwelling place with him." Because of the indwelling Holy Spirit, we have the opportunity with the spiritual eyes of our heart to be in *face-to-face* fellowship with our Lord. The result is glory.

Glory is another important quality in the life of one who is personally, spiritually revived. The Hebrew word is *kabod* and means the reality and splendor of God's presence. God's great goal is to make known His glory. In other words, His intention is that you would experience the reality and splendor of His presence. Psalm 19 begins, "The heavens declare the glory of God" (NIV). God created the heavens and earth that you might catch a glimpse of His presence. His glory filled the Old Testament temple. He has always intended to dwell with us so that we might experience the splendor of His presence.

The most complete demonstration of His glory is Jesus Christ: "The Word became flesh, and dwelt among us, and we saw His glory, glory as of the only begotten from the Father, full of grace and truth" (John 1:14). In Jesus we experience God's presence. That experience changes us more and more into His likeness. As you experience Jesus' presence, you will become more and more like Him. His glory will transform you. "But we all, with unveiled face, beholding as in a mirror the glory of the Lord, are being transformed into the same image from glory to glory, just as from the Lord, the Spirit" (2 Corinthians 3:18). "For God who said, 'Light shall shine out of darkness' is the One who has shone in our hearts to give the Light of the knowledge of the glory of God in the face of Christ" (2 Corinthians 4:6). You are the light of the world because of the presence of God that is shining out from within you. His presence changes you and those around you. The transforming power of His glory is ignited when you have a face-to-face friendship with your Lord.

READ AND STUDY GOD'S WORD

1. The life of revival includes an intimate relationship with God that produces a new kind of sight. What do you learn about this new kind of sight from the following verses?
2 Corinthians 4:18

Ephesians 1:18-19

Hebrews 12:1-2

2. How does what we see affect us?
2 Corinthians 3:18

2 Corinthians 4:6-7

1 John 3:2-3

3. According to Revelation 22:3-4, what will we see in heaven?

ADORE GOD IN PRAYER

O you, who are the brightness of your Father's glory and the exact image of his person, may I catch some of that brightness and manifest some of that image, that people
may turn from my reflection to you, the eternal reality.[1]

F. B. MEYER IN *DAILY PRAYERS*

YIELD YOURSELF TO GOD

To state it in brief, I would just say that man's part is to trust and God's part is to work;
and it can be seen at a glance how contrastive these two parts are, and yet not necessarily contradictory. I mean this. There is a certain work to be accomplished. We are
to be delivered from the power of sin, and are to be made perfect in every good work
to do the will of God. "Beholding as in a glass the glory of the Lord," we are to be actually "changed into the same image from glory to glory, even as by the Spirit of the
Lord." We are to be transformed by the renewing of our minds, that we may prove what
is that good and acceptable and perfect will of God. A real work is to be wrought in us
and upon us. Besetting sins are to be conquered. Evil habits are to be overcome. Wrong
dispositions and feelings are to be rooted out, and holy tempers and emotions are to
be begotten. A positive transformation is to take place. So at least the Bible teaches.
Now somebody must do this. Either we must do it for ourselves, or another must do it
for us. We have most of us tried to do it for ourselves at first, and have grievously failed;
then we discover from the Scriptures and from our own experience that it is a work we
are utterly unable to do for ourselves, but that the Lord Jesus Christ has come on purpose to do it, and that He will do it for all who put themselves wholly into His hand,
and trust Him to do it. Now under these circumstances, what is the part of the believer,
and what is the part of the Lord? Plainly the believer can do nothing but trust; while
the Lord, in whom he trusts, actually does the work entrusted to Him.

HANNAH WHITALL SMITH IN *THE CHRISTIAN'S SECRET OF A HAPPY LIFE*

The man who gazes upon and contemplates day by day the face of the Lord Jesus
Christ, and who has caught the glow of the reality that the Lord is not a theory but an
indwelling power and force in his life, is as a mirror reflecting the glory of the Lord.
Wherever he goes, people begin to ask questions as to why he triumphs when others
fail; why it is when at business everything is at sixes and sevens and all is upset and con-
fused, he maintains a sense of poise; how it is, when facing buffeting of one kind or another, he reacts with such patience; how it is, when the general level of conversation is
so impure he is never dragged down, and how he stands above it, not in a sense of
rebuke to others but in a sense of testimony to the fact that, because he belongs to
God, he cannot descend to another level. He has caught the glow and is reflecting it.[2]

ALAN REDPATH IN *BLESSINGS OUT OF BUFFETINGS*

Revival and blessing come to the church when we stop looking at a picture of God and look at God Himself. Revival comes when, no longer satisfied just to know about a God in history, we meet the conditions of finding Him in living, personal experience. Conversely, revival cannot come if we are far removed from God. It cannot come if, instead of hearing His voice, we are content with only an echo. Put those deficiencies together and you have the reason why we are so dissatisfied and empty. You have the reason why there is so little of vivid, vibrant joy in the things of God. Do you think Abraham would have accomplished what he did in the realm of faith if he had declined his notable face-to-face encounter with God? What would have been Moses' biography had he not experienced God personally? Jacob lost his reputation as a deceiver and a supplanter and became Israel, "one who prevails with God," when he encountered God at Peniel. It was then that he could say, "I have seen God face to face, and my life is preserved." Go to Isaiah 6 and you will find the confession of the great prophet who wrote that book under God's inspiration. It was not until he experienced a dramatic confrontation with the Lord of heaven and earth that he was transformed with reverent awe, humility and cleansing. Only then could he say, "Here am I; send me."[3]

A. W. TOZER IN *MEN WHO MET GOD*

ENJOY HIS PRESENCE
Think about how you see the Lord without your physical eyes. Is your life characterized by a face-to-face friendship with your Lord? What can you do today to cultivate that friendship and grow in intimacy with Him so that you might reflect His glory?

Close your time with the Lord by meditating on this prayer by A. W. Tozer:

Lord, I would trust Thee completely; I would be altogether Thine; I would exalt Thee above all. I desire that I may feel no sense of possessing anything outside of Thee. I want constantly to be aware of Thy overshadowing Presence and to hear Thy speaking Voice. I long to live in restful sincerity of heart. I want to live so fully in the Spirit that all my thoughts may be as sweet incense ascending to Thee and every act of my life may be an act of worship. Therefore I pray in the words of Thy great servant of old, "I beseech Thee so for to cleanse the intent of mine heart with the unspeakable gift of Thy grace, that I may perfectly love Thee and worthily praise Thee." And all this I confidently believe Thou wilt grant me through the merits of Jesus Christ Thy Son. Amen.[4]

A. W. TOZER IN *THE PURSUIT OF GOD*

REST IN HIS LOVE
"Do everything without complaining or arguing, so that you may become blameless and pure, children of God without fault in a crooked and depraved generation, in which you shine like stars in the universe" (Philippians 2:14-15, NIV).

worship

Seven times a day I praise You.
PSALM 119:164

Prepare Your Heart

It always seems sad to leave any study after having spent so much time with the Lord in one place. Psalm 119 has been our place of meeting with the Lord for many days. What a rich time it has been! The circumstances were extreme for this psalmist and moved him to pray the longest prayer in the Bible. However, this psalm has trained us in personal spiritual revival. His prayer for revival has been our challenge. In this final day on personal spiritual revival, it is fitting that we look at the very highest experience of revival: worship.

To worship God is to pour out your heart of love and adoration for your Lord with utter abandon. Your whole life is to be clothed in worship. It is the natural result of intimacy with the Lord. God wants to fill your heart with praise and worship. In Psalm 119:175, the psalmist said, "Let my soul live that it may praise You." The Hebrew word for praise in verse 175 is *balal* and means to be bright, to shine, to be splendid, and to celebrate. This is your natural response to God. To know God is to praise Him.

As you begin your time with the Lord, meditate on this hymn by Reginald Heber:

> Holy, holy, holy! Lord God Almighty!
> Early in the morning our song shall rise to thee.
> Holy, holy, holy! Merciful and mighty,
> God in three persons, blessed Trinity!
>
> Holy, holy, holy! All the saints adore thee,
> casting down their golden crowns around the glassy sea;
> cherubim and seraphim falling down before thee,
> which wert, and art, and evermore shalt be.

Holy, holy, holy! Though the darkness hide thee,
though the eye of sinful man thy glory may not see,
only thou art holy; there is none beside thee,
perfect in power, in love and purity.

Holy, holy, holy! Lord God Almighty!
All thy works shall praise thy name, in earth and sky and sea.
Holy, holy, holy! Merciful and mighty,
God in three persons, blessed Trinity.

READ AND STUDY GOD'S WORD

1. One of the best examples of worship with abandon is seen in the woman who bathed Jesus' feet with perfume. Read Luke 7:37-50. Meditate on it. How did she worship Jesus? Make as many observations about her expression of love for Jesus as you can.

Do you worship Him with such love and abandon? What helps or hinders you?

2. As God reveals His ways and character to you, you will be led to worship Him more and more. Look at the following verses and record what you see about God that causes you to worship Him.

1 Samuel 2:2

1 Chronicles 29:11-13

Psalm 84:11

Isaiah 63:7-9

Lamentations 3:21-25

Zephaniah 3:17

3. What is your favorite truth about God that causes you to worship Him today?

ADORE GOD IN PRAYER

Turn to the Lord now, and place yourself and your desires in His hands. You may want to use the following prayer, taken from *31 Days of Praise* by Ruth Myers.

Lord, I'm Yours. Whatever the cost may be, may Your will be done in my life. I realize I'm not here on earth to do my own thing, or to seek my own fulfillment or my own glory. I'm not here to indulge my desires, to increase my possessions, to impress people, to be popular, to prove I'm somebody important, or to promote myself. I'm not here even to be relevant or successful by human standards. I'm here to please You.

I offer myself to You, for You are worthy. All that I am or hope to be, I owe to You. I'm Yours by creation, and every day I receive from You life and breath and all things. And I'm Yours because You bought me, and the price You paid was the precious blood of Christ. You alone, the Triune God, are worthy to be my Lord and Master. I yield to You, my gracious and glorious heavenly Father, to the Lord Jesus who loved me and gave Himself for me, to the Holy Spirit and His gracious influence and empowering. All that I am and all that I have I give to You.

I give You any rebellion in me, that resists doing Your will. I give You my pride and self-dependence, that tell me I can do Your will in my own power if I try hard enough. I give You my fears, that tell me I'll never be able to do Your will in some areas of life. I consent to let You energize me . . . to create within me, moment by moment, both the desire and the power to do Your will.

I give You my body and each of its members . . . my entire inner being: my mind, my emotional life, my will . . . my loved ones . . . my marriage or my hopes for marriage . . . my abilities and gifts . . . my strengths and weaknesses . . . my health . . . my status (high or low) . . . my possessions . . . my past, my present and my future . . . when and how I'll go Home.

I'm here to love You, to obey You, to glorify You. Oh my Beloved, may I be a joy to You![1]

YIELD YOURSELF TO GOD

To speak of the *deeper life* is not to speak of anything deeper than simple New Testament religion. Rather it is to insist that believers explore the depths of the Christian evangel for those riches it surely contains but which we are as surely missing. The *deeper life* is deeper only because the average Christian life is tragically shallow. . . . What the deeper life advocates are telling us is that we should press on to enjoy in personal inward experience the exalted privileges that are ours in Christ Jesus; that we should insist upon tasting the sweetness of internal worship in spirit as well as in truth; that to reach this ideal we should if necessary push beyond our contented brethren and bring upon ourselves whatever opposition may follow as a result.[2]

A. W. TOZER IN *LEANING INTO THE WIND*

Worship flows from love. Where love is meager, worship will be scant. Where love is deep, worship will overflow. As Paul wrote his letters, his contemplation of the love and glory of God would spontaneously cause his heart to overflow in worship and doxology. . . . Worship is the loving ascription of praise to God, for what He is in Himself and in His providential dealings. It is the bowing of our innermost spirit before Him in deepest humility and reverence. . . . In the Bible, we have the full and adequate revelation of the vast scope of the divine nature. Great tracts of truth await our exploration. Great themes—God's sovereignty, truth, holiness, wisdom, love, faithfulness, patience, mercy—illumined and made relevant to us by the Holy Spirit, will feed the flame of our worship.[3]

J. OSWALD SANDERS IN *ENJOYING INTIMACY WITH GOD*

Worship often includes words and actions, but it goes beyond them to the *focus* of the mind and heart. Worship is the God-centered focus and response of the inner man; it is being preoccupied with God. So no matter what you are saying or singing or doing at any moment, you are worshiping God only when you are focused on Him and thinking of Him.[4]

DONALD WHITNEY IN *SPIRITUAL DISCIPLINES FOR THE CHRISTIAN LIFE*

All of our victories, whether they result in an instantaneous deliverance from a circumstance or are simply the strength to endure a long and difficult trial, flow from God's nature and character alone. God's presence is our victory and praise makes room for the fullness of God.[5]

DICK EASTMAN IN *A CELEBRATION OF PRAISE*

ENJOY HIS PRESENCE

The psalmist said "Seven times a day I praise You, because of Your righteous ordinances" (Psalm 119:164). What are ways in which you can praise the Lord throughout the day?

In the house of God there is never-ending festival; the angel choir makes eternal holi-day; the presence of God's face gives joy that never fails. And from that everlasting, perpetual festivity there sounds in the ears of the heart a strain, mysterious, melodious, sweet—provided the world does not drown it.

ST. AUGUSTINE IN *PATROLOGIA LATINA*

Consider kneeling before the Lord today (following the example of the psalmist in Psalm 95:6-7) and worshiping Him for who He is. You looked at passages today that reveal the ways and character of your Lord. You may choose to use the words that you have written from Scripture to worship the Lord today.

REST IN HIS LOVE

"Come, let us bow down in worship, let us kneel before the LORD our Maker, for he is our God and we are the people of his pasture, the flock under his care" (Psalm 95:6-7, NIV).

DEAR FRIEND,

1. We come now to the end of our quiet times on personal spiritual revival. Turn back to the first day of the first week. You wrote a letter to the Lord, asking Him to speak to you during this study. Read that letter. How has He answered your prayer?

2. What is the most important truth you will take with you from this study on personal spiritual revival?

3. What is your understanding of the kind of life that is possible for you as a believer in Jesus Christ? What does it mean to be personally, spiritually revived?

4. What was your favorite quote in this study?

5. Who was your favorite example in these quiet times? Why do you choose that person?

6. What prayer from Psalm 119 will you remember the most?

7. What was your favorite chapter in this study on personal spiritual revival, and why?

8. Finally, what is the verse you will remember from your study on personal spiritual revival?

Close with a prayer of worship and thanksgiving to your Lord.

If awakenings of the past foreshadow events to come, I believe we will see the fire of the Holy Spirit break out in the churches and spread to every nook and cranny in the land. We will see revival begin with God's people, but millions of unbelievers every-where—in government, education, the media, Hollywood—will turn to Christ in unprecedented numbers. That is the nature of true revival. It is never contained within church walls. As this revival sweeps throughout our nation and around the world, we will see renewed religious fervor. There will be a fresh awareness of the awesomeness of God and His other attributes, a restoration of true worship, a hunger for the Word of God, and a new zeal to help fulfill the Great Commission, telling others about our Lord Jesus Christ and the good news of God's love and forgiveness.[1]

DR. BILL BRIGHT IN *THE COMING REVIVAL*

In the midst of this great chill there are some, I rejoice to acknowledge, who will not be content with shallow logic. They will admit the force of the argument, and then turn away with tears to hunt some lonely place and pray, *O God, show me Thy glory.* They want to taste, to touch with their hearts, to see with their inner eyes the wonder that is God.[2]

A. W. TOZER IN *THE PURSUIT OF GOD*

Close by thinking about this reading from *Streams in the Desert:*

They were living to themselves; self with its hopes, and promises and dreams, still had hold of them; but the Lord began to fulfill their prayers. They had asked for contrition, and had surrendered for it to be given them at any cost, and He sent them sorrow; they had asked for purity, and He sent them thrilling anguish; they had asked to be meek, and He had broken their hearts; they had asked to be dead to the world, and He slew all their living hopes; they had asked to be made like unto Him, and He placed them in the furnace, sitting by *as a refiner and purifier of silver,* until they should reflect His image; they had asked to lay hold of His cross, and when He had reached it to them it lacerated their hands.

They had asked they knew not what, nor how, but He had taken them at their word, and granted them all their petitions. They were hardly willing to follow Him so far, or to draw so nigh to Him. They had upon them an awe and fear, as Jacob at Bethel, or Eliphaz in the night visions, or as the apostles when they thought that they had seen a spirit, and knew not that it was Jesus. They could almost pray Him to depart from them, or to hide His awfulness. They found it easier to obey than to suffer, to do than to give up, to bear the cross than to hang upon it. But they cannot go back, for they have come too near the unseen cross, and its virtues have pierced too deeply within them. He is fulfilling to them His promise *And I, if I be lifted up from the earth, will draw all men unto Me* (John 12:32).

But now at last their turn has come. Before, they had only heard of the mystery, but now they feel it. He has fastened on them His look of love, as He did on Mary and Peter, and they can but choose to follow.

Little by little, from time to time, by fitting gleams, the mystery of His cross shines out upon them. They behold Him lifted up, they gaze on the glory rays from the wounds of His holy passion; and as they gaze they advance, and are changed into His likeness, and His name shines out through them, for He dwells in them. They live alone with Him above in unspeakable fellowship; willing to lack what others own, (and what they might have had), and to be unlike all, so that they are only like Him.

Such are they in all ages *who follow the Lamb withersoever He goeth*.

Had they chosen for themselves, or their friends chosen for them, they would have chosen otherwise. They would have been brighter here, but less glorious in His kingdom. They would have had Lot's portion, not Abraham's. If they had halted anywhere—if God had taken off His hand and let them stray back—what would they not have lost? What forfeits in the resurrection?

But He stayed them up, even against themselves. Many a time their foot had well nigh slipped; but He in mercy held them up. Now, even in this life, they know that all He did was done well. It was good to suffer here, that they might reign hereafter; to bear the cross below, for they wear the crown above; and that not their will but His was done on them and in them.[3]

ANONYMOUS IN *STREAMS IN THE DESERT*

Therefore if you have been raised up with Christ, keep seeking the things above, where Christ is, seated at the right hand of God. Set your mind on the things above, not on the things that are on earth. For you have died and your life is hidden with Christ in God. When Christ, who is our life, is revealed, then you also will be revealed with Him in glory. (Colossians 3:1-4)

Things which eye has not seen and ear has not heard,
And which have not entered the heart of man,
All that God has prepared for those who love Him. (1 Corinthians 2:9)

now that you have completed these quiet times

You have spent nine weeks consistently drawing near to God in quiet time with Him. That time alone with Him does not need to come to an end. What is the next step? To continue your pursuit of God, you might consider other books of quiet times in this series, including *Pilgrimage of the Heart: Satisfy Your Longing for Adventure with God* and *A Heart That Dances: Satisfy Your Desire for Intimacy with God*.

You might choose to meet with friends as you spend time with the Lord using these books. Leader's guides, audiotapes and videotapes are available to accompany each book. Apply practical ideas on how to have a quiet time, including choosing a Bible reading plan, setting aside a time and a place, using devotional books, and recording your insights in a quiet time notebook or journal. Quiet Time Ministries™ has many resources to encourage you in your quiet time with God, including the Quiet Time Notebook, *Enriching Your Quiet Time* magazine, audiotapes, and videotapes. These resources may be ordered online from Quiet Time Ministries at www.quiettime.org. You may also call Quiet Time Ministries to order or request a catalog.

For more information, you may contact:

Quiet Time Ministries™
P.O. Box 14007
Palm Desert, California 92255
(800) 925-6458, (760) 772-2357
E-mail: catherine@quiettime.org
www.quiettime.org.

Pour out your heart like water in the presence of the Lord.
LAMENTATIONS 2:19, NIV

Pour out your heart like water in the presence of the Lord.
LAMENTATIONS 2:19, NIV

Pour out your heart like water in the presence of the Lord.
LAMENTATIONS 2:19, NIV

Pour out your heart like water in the presence of the Lord.
LAMENTATIONS 2:19, NIV

Pour out your heart like water in the presence of the Lord.
LAMENTATIONS 2:19, NIV

Pour out your heart like water in the presence of the Lord.
LAMENTATIONS 2:19, NIV

Pour out your heart like water in the presence of the Lord.
LAMENTATIONS 2:19, NIV

Pour out your heart like water in the presence of the Lord.
LAMENTATIONS 2:19, NIV

Pour out your heart like water in the presence of the Lord.
LAMENTATIONS 2:19, NIV

_____

_____

_____

_____

_____

_____

_____

_____

_____

_____

_____

_____

_____

_____

_____

_____

Pour out your heart like water in the presence of the Lord.
LAMENTATIONS 2:19, NIV

Pour out your heart like water in the presence of the Lord.
LAMENTATIONS 2:19, NIV

Pour out your heart like water in the presence of the Lord.
LAMENTATIONS 2:19, NIV

Pour out your heart like water in the presence of the Lord.
LAMENTATIONS 2:19, NIV

Pour out your heart like water in the presence of the Lord.
LAMENTATIONS 2:19, NIV

_____

_____

_____

_____

_____

_____

_____

_____

_____

_____

_____

_____

_____

_____

_____

Do not be anxious about anything, but in everything, by prayer and petition, with thanksgiving, present your requests to God. And the peace of God, which transcends all understanding, will guard your hearts and your minds in Christ Jesus.

PHILIPPIANS 4:6-7, NIV

PRAYER FOR _____

DATE:

SCRIPTURE:

REQUEST:

ANSWER:

PRAYER FOR _____

DATE:

SCRIPTURE:

REQUEST:

ANSWER:

Do not be anxious about anything, but in everything, by prayer and petition, with thanksgiving, present your requests to God. And the peace of God, which transcends all understanding, will guard your hearts and your minds in Christ Jesus.

PHILIPPIANS 4:6-7, NIV

PRAYER FOR _____

DATE:

SCRIPTURE:

REQUEST:

ANSWER:

PRAYER FOR _____

DATE:

SCRIPTURE:

REQUEST:

ANSWER:

Do not be anxious about anything, but in everything, by prayer and petition, with thanksgiving, present your requests to God. And the peace of God, which transcends all understanding, will guard your hearts and your minds in Christ Jesus.
PHILIPPIANS 4:6-7, NIV

PRAYER FOR _____

DATE:

SCRIPTURE:

REQUEST:

ANSWER:

PRAYER FOR _____

DATE:

SCRIPTURE:

REQUEST:

ANSWER:

Do not be anxious about anything, but in everything, by prayer and petition, with thanksgiving, present your requests to God. And the peace of God, which transcends all understanding, will guard your hearts and your minds in Christ Jesus.
PHILIPPIANS 4:6-7, NIV

PRAYER FOR _____

DATE:

SCRIPTURE:

REQUEST:

ANSWER:

PRAYER FOR _____

DATE:

SCRIPTURE:

REQUEST:

ANSWER:

Do not be anxious about anything, but in everything, by prayer and petition, with thanksgiving, present your requests to God. And the peace of God, which transcends all understanding, will guard your hearts and your minds in Christ Jesus.
PHILIPPIANS 4:6-7, NIV

PRAYER FOR _____

DATE:

SCRIPTURE:

REQUEST:

ANSWER:

PRAYER FOR _____

DATE:

SCRIPTURE:

REQUEST:

ANSWER:

Do not be anxious about anything, but in everything, by prayer and petition, with thanksgiving, present your requests to God. And the peace of God, which transcends all understanding, will guard your hearts and your minds in Christ Jesus.
PHILIPPIANS 4:6-7, NIV

PRAYER FOR _____

DATE:

SCRIPTURE:

REQUEST:

ANSWER:

PRAYER FOR _____

DATE:

SCRIPTURE:

REQUEST:

ANSWER:

Do not be anxious about anything, but in everything, by prayer and petition, with thanksgiving, present your requests to God. And the peace of God, which transcends all understanding, will guard your hearts and your minds in Christ Jesus.
PHILIPPIANS 4:6-7, NIV

PRAYER FOR _____

DATE:

SCRIPTURE:

REQUEST:

ANSWER:

PRAYER FOR _____

DATE:

SCRIPTURE:

REQUEST:

ANSWER:

Do not be anxious about anything, but in everything, by prayer and petition, with thanksgiving, present your requests to God. And the peace of God, which transcends all understanding, will guard your hearts and your minds in Christ Jesus.
PHILIPPIANS 4:6-7, NIV

PRAYER FOR _____

DATE:

SCRIPTURE:

REQUEST:

ANSWER:

PRAYER FOR _____

DATE:

SCRIPTURE:

REQUEST:

ANSWER:

Do not be anxious about anything, but in everything, by prayer and petition, with thanksgiving, present your requests to God. And the peace of God, which transcends all understanding, will guard your hearts and your minds in Christ Jesus.
PHILIPPIANS 4:6-7, NIV

PRAYER FOR _____

DATE:

SCRIPTURE:

REQUEST:

ANSWER:

PRAYER FOR _____

DATE:

SCRIPTURE:

REQUEST:

ANSWER:

Do not be anxious about anything, but in everything, by prayer and petition, with thanksgiving, present your requests to God. And the peace of God, which transcends all understanding, will guard your hearts and your minds in Christ Jesus.

PHILIPPIANS 4:6-7, NIV

PRAYER FOR _____

DATE:

SCRIPTURE:

REQUEST:

ANSWER:

PRAYER FOR _____

DATE:

SCRIPTURE:

REQUEST:

ANSWER:

Do not be anxious about anything, but in everything, by prayer and petition, with thanksgiving, present your requests to God. And the peace of God, which transcends all understanding, will guard your hearts and your minds in Christ Jesus.
PHILIPPIANS 4:6-7, NIV

PRAYER FOR _____

DATE:

SCRIPTURE:

REQUEST:

ANSWER:

PRAYER FOR _____

DATE:

SCRIPTURE:

REQUEST:

ANSWER:

Do not be anxious about anything, but in everything, by prayer and petition, with thanksgiving, present your requests to God. And the peace of God, which transcends all understanding, will guard your hearts and your minds in Christ Jesus.
PHILIPPIANS 4:6-7, NIV

PRAYER FOR _____

DATE:

SCRIPTURE:

REQUEST:

ANSWER:

PRAYER FOR _____

DATE:

SCRIPTURE:

REQUEST:

ANSWER:

Do not be anxious about anything, but in everything, by prayer and petition, with thanksgiving, present your requests to God. And the peace of God, which transcends all understanding, will guard your hearts and your minds in Christ Jesus.
PHILIPPIANS 4:6-7, NIV

PRAYER FOR _____

DATE:

SCRIPTURE:

REQUEST:

ANSWER:

PRAYER FOR _____

DATE:

SCRIPTURE:

REQUEST:

ANSWER:

Do not be anxious about anything, but in everything, by prayer and petition, with thanksgiving, present your requests to God. And the peace of God, which transcends all understanding, will guard your hearts and your minds in Christ Jesus.
PHILIPPIANS 4:6-7, NIV

PRAYER FOR _____

DATE:

SCRIPTURE:

REQUEST:

ANSWER:

PRAYER FOR _____

DATE:

SCRIPTURE:

REQUEST:

ANSWER:

notes

INTRODUCTION

1. Used by permission of Quiet Time Ministries.

WEEK 1, DAY 1

1. Herbert F. Stevenson, ed., *Keswick's Authentic Voice* (London: Marshall, Morgan & Scott, 1959), pp. 313-314.

WEEK 1, DAY 2

1. Taken from *Jesus Man Of Joy.* Copyright © 1999 by Sherwood E. Wirt. Published by Harvest House Publishers, Eugene, Oregon 97402. Used by permission. Page 36.

2. Charles W. Slemming, *He Restoreth My Soul*, The Quiet Hour Series (London: Henry E. Walter, Ltd., n.d.), p. 1.

WEEK 1, DAY 3

1. Leon Morris, *The Gospel According to John: The New International Commentary on the New Testament* (Grand Rapids, Mich.: Eerdmans, 1971), pp. 419-426.

2. Herbert F. Stevenson, ed., *Keswick's Authentic Voice* (London: Marshall, Morgan & Scott, 1959), p. 457.

WEEK 1, DAY 4

1. A. W. Tozer, *The Pursuit of God* (Camp Hill, Penn.: Christian Publications, 1993), p. 91. Used by permission. For more information on these and other books by A. W. Tozer, call 1-800-233-4443 or visit Christian Publications' website at www.christianpublications.com.

2. Andrew Murray, *With Christ in the School of Prayer* (Old Tappan, N.J.: Fleming H. Revell, a division of Baker Book House Company, 1953), p. 67.

WEEK 1, DAY 5

1. Evan Hopkins, "The Fulness Of The Spirit" in Herbert F. Stevenson, ed., *Keswick's Authentic Voice* (London: Marshall, Morgan & Scott, 1959), p. 464.

2. F. B. Meyer, *Gospel of John* (Fort Washington, Penn.: Christian Literature Crusade, 1970), p. 117. Used by permission.

WEEK 1, DAYS 6–7

1. F. B. Meyer, *Gospel of John* (Fort Washington, Penn.: Christian Literature Crusade, 1970), p. 120. Used by permission.

WEEK 2, DAY 1

1. Dr. and Mrs. Taylor, *Hudson Taylor's Spiritual Secret* (Chicago: Moody, 1989).
2. John Piper, *The Pleasures of God* (Portland, Ore.: Multnomah, 1991), pp. 187-188. Used by permission.

WEEK 2, DAY 2

1. Charles Spurgeon, *Morning and Evening* (Scotland: Christian Focus Publications, 1994), Dec. 18, morning.
2. Zac Poonen, *Beauty for Ashes* (Bombay: Gospel Literature Service, 1973), pp. 20-22. Used by permission of author.
3. Andrew Murray, *Humility* (Fort Washington, Penn.: Christian Literature Crusade, 1980), pp. 98-99. Used by permission.
4. Charles Spurgeon, *Morning and Evening* (Scotland: Christian Focus Publications, 1994), Dec. 16, morning.

WEEK 2, DAY 3

1. Reprinted from *Daily Prayers*. Copyright © 1995 by F. B. Meyer. Harold Shaw Publishers, an imprint of WaterBrook Press, Colorado Springs, Colo. All rights reserved. Page 42.
2. Charles Spurgeon, *Morning and Evening* (Scotland: Christian Focus Publications, 1994), April 4, evening.
3. A. W. Tozer, *The Pursuit of God* (Camp Hill, Penn.: Christian Publications, 1993), p. 56. Used by permission. For more information on these and other books by A. W. Tozer, call 1-800-233-4443 or visit Christian Publications' website at www.christianpublications.com.

WEEK 2, DAY 4

1. R. Laird Harris, Gleason L. Archer Jr., and Bruce K. Waltke, eds., *Theological Wordbook of the Old Testament*, vol. 2 (Chicago: Moody, 1980), p. 909.
2. A. W. Tozer, *The Pursuit of God* (Camp Hill, Penn.: Christian Publications, 1993), p. 110. Used by permission. For more information on these and other books by A. W. Tozer, call 1-800-233-4443 or visit Christian Publications' website at www.christianpublications.com.
3. Taken from INNER LIFE, THE by Andrew Murray. Copyright © 1980 by Zondervan Corporation. Used by permission of Zondervan Publishing House. Pages 68-69.

WEEK 2, DAY 5

1. Norman Grubb, *Continuous Revival* (Fort Washington, Penn.: Christian Literature Crusade, 1996), p. 45. Used by permission.
2. Alan Redpath, *The Making of a Man of God* (Old Tappan, N.J.: Fleming H. Revell, a division of Baker Book House Company, 1962), pp. 192-193. Used by permission.

WEEK 2, DAYS 6–7

1. From *Revival* by D. Martyn Lloyd-Jones, copyright © 1987, pages 154-155. Used by permission of Crossway Books, a division of Good News Publishers, Wheaton, Illinois 60187.

WEEK 3, DAY 1

1. From Elizabeth R. Skoglund, *Amma: The Life and Words of Amy Carmichael* (Grand Rapids, Mich.: Raven's Ridge Books, a division of Baker Book House, 1994), p. 15.
2. Amy Carmichael, *Gold by Moonlight* (Fort Washington, Penn.: Christian Literature Crusade, n.d.), pp. 153-154. Used by permission.

WEEK 3, DAY 2

1. Amy Carmichael, *Gold by Moonlight* (Fort Washington, Penn.: Christian Literature Crusade, n.d.), p. 98. Used by permission.

WEEK 3, DAY 3

1. J. J. Stewart Perowne, *Commentary on the Psalms* (1878-1879; reprint Grand Rapids, Mich.: Kregel Publications, 1989), pp. 347-348.

WEEK 3, DAY 4

1. Amy Carmichael, *Overweights of Joy* (New York: Revell, n.d.), p. 300.

WEEK 3, DAY 5

1. R. B. Jones, *Rent Heavens*, from www.revival-library.org/jonesrb/92.html
2. Amy Carmichael, *Toward Jerusalem* (Fort Washington, Penn.: Christian Literature Crusade, 1936), p. 17. Used by permission.
3. Charles Spurgeon, *Morning and Evening* (Scotland: Christian Focus Publications, 1994), June 10, morning.

WEEK 3, DAYS 6–7

1. Brian H. Edwards, *Revival: A People Saturated with God* (Darlington, England: Evangelical Press, 1990), pp. 46-48. Used by permission.

WEEK 4, DAY 1

1. Ruth Paxson, *Life on the Highest Plane* (Chicago: Moody, 1928).
2. Norman Grubb, *Continuous Revival* (Fort Washington, Penn.: Christian Literature Crusade, 1996), pp. 6-7. Used by permission.

WEEK 4, DAY 2

1. *The Shadow of the Broad Brim: The Life Story of Charles Haddon Spurgeon* by Richard Ellsworth Day © 1934 by Judson Press, Valley Forge, Penn. Page 138. Used by permission.
2. Taken from *Matthew Henry's Commentary of the Whole Bible* by Leslie F. Church; Gerald W. Peterman. Copyright © 1991 by Harper Collins Publishers Ltd. Used by permission of Zondervan Publishing House. Page 1555.

WEEK 4, DAY 3

1. Matthew 25:23 (NIV).
2. A. W. Tozer, *The Pursuit of God* (Camp Hill, Penn.: Christian Publications, 1993), p. 13. Used by permission. For more information on these and other books by A. W. Tozer, call 1-800-233-4443 or visit Christian Publications' website at www.christianpublications.com.

Week 4, Day 4

1. Spiros Zodhiates, *The Complete Word Study Old Testament* (Chattanooga, Tenn.: AMG Publishers, 1994), p. 2357.

Week 4, Day 5

1. Darlene Diebler Rose, *Evidence Not Seen* (San Francisco: Harper, 1990).
2. Brennan Manning, *The Signature of Jesus* (Sisters, Ore.: Multnomah, 1988), pp. 139-140. Used by permission.
3. Charles Spurgeon, "Love and I—A Mystery," No. 1667, delivered July 2, 1882, at the Metropolitan Tabernacle, Newington, England.

Week 4, Days 6–7

1. Charles Spurgeon, *The Treasury of David*, vol. 3 (McLean, VA: MacDonald Publishing Company, n.d.), pp. 189-190.

Week 5, Day 1

1. Taken from *Living by the Book* by Howard G. and William D. Hendricks, Moody Press, copyright 1991. Used with permission. Page 9.
2. Taken from *Living by the Book* by Howard G. and William D. Hendricks, Moody Press, copyright 1991. Used with permission. Page 5.
3. From the foreword of *What the Bible Is All About* by Henrietta C. Mears. Copyright 1983. Gospel Light/Regal Books, Ventura, CA 93003. Used by permission.

Week 5, Day 2

1. John Woodbridge, ed., *More Than Conquerors* (Chicago: Moody, 1992), pp. 143-144.
2. Rev. F. S. Schenk, *The Bible Reader's Guide* (New York: American Tract Society, 1896), from the Introduction, "How to Study the Bible," by D. L. Moody, p. i.
3. Permission to copy was granted by Banner Of Truth, Carlisle, Penn., and taken from the book *The Valley of Vision*, Arthur Bennett, ed. Page 17.
4. Schenk, pp. ii, x.

Week 5, Day 3

1. Charles Spurgeon, *Morning and Evening* (Scotland: Christian Focus Publications, 1994), Dec. 9, evening.
2. Herbert Lockyer Sr., *Psalms: A Devotional Commentary* (Grand Rapids, Mich.: Kregel Publications, 1993), pp. 539-541.
3. Lockyer, pp. 539-541.
4. Reprinted from *Psalms: The Prayer Book of the Bible* by Dietrich Bonhoeffer, © 1970 Augsburg Publishing House. Used by permission of Augsburg Fortress. Pages 31-32.

Week 5, Day 4

1. J. H. Merle D'Aubigne, *The Life and Times of Martin Luther* (Chicago: Moody, n.d.), p. 65.
2. Taken from *The Inner Life*, by Andrew Murray. Copyright © 1980 by Zondervan Corporation. Used by permission of Zondervan Publishing House. Pages 20-23.

WEEK 5, DAY 5

1. Spiros Zodhiates, *The Complete Word Study Old Testament* (Chattanooga, Tenn.: AMG Publishers, 1994), p. 2373.
2. Merrill C. Tenney, *Galatians: The Charter of Christian Liberty* (Grand Rapids, Mich.: Wm. B. Eerdmans Publishing Company, 1950), pp. 207-208. Used by permission.
3. Josh McDowell, *Guide to Understanding Your Bible* (San Bernardino, Calif.: Here's Life Publishers, 1982), pp. 8-9.
4. Taken from *The Inner Life*, by Andrew Murray. Copyright © 1980 by Zondervan Corporation. Used by permission of Zondervan Publishing House. Pages 42-44.

WEEK 5, DAYS 6–7

1. Charles Bridges, *Psalm 119* (Carlisle, Penn.: Banner Of Truth Trust, 1827), pp. 124-125.

WEEK 6, DAY 1

1. Kenneth Wuest, *Wuest's Word Studies*, vol. 2 (Grand Rapids, Mich.: Wm. B. Eerdmans Publishing Company, 1973), p. 128. Used by permission.
2. Wuest, p. 128. Used by permission.
3. Reprinted from UNDER HIS WINGS by O. Hallesby, © 1932 Augsburg Publishing House. Used by permission of Augsburg Fortress. Page 32.
4. Alan Redpath, *Faith for the Times* (Grand Rapids, Mich.: Fleming H. Revell, a division of Baker Book House Company, 1972), page 58. Used by permission.
5. Annie Johnson Flint, "The Pruned Branch" in *Poems* (Toronto: Evangelical Publishers, 1944).

WEEK 6, DAY 2

1. This material is taken from *Christian Discipline* by Oswald Chambers. Copyright © 1935, 1936, 1995 by the Oswald Chambers Publications Assn., Ltd. Originally published by Zondervan Publishers ©1985. Used by permission of Discovery House Publishers, Box 3566, Grand Rapids, Mich. 49501. All rights reserved. Page 68.
2. This material is taken from *Christian Discipline* by Oswald Chambers. Copyright © 1935, 1936, 1995 by the Oswald Chambers Publications Assn., Ltd. Originally published by Zondervan Publishers ©1985. Used by permission of Discovery House Publishers, Box 3566, Grand Rapids, Mich. 49501. All rights reserved. Page 76.

WEEK 6, DAY 3

1. Reprinted from *Daily Prayers*. Copyright © 1995 by F. B. Meyer, Harold Shaw Publishers, an imprint of WaterBrook Press, Colorado Springs, CO. All rights reserved. Page 54.
2. Taken from *The Blessings of Brokenness*, by Charles F. Stanley. Copyright © 1997 by Charles F. Stanley. Used by permission of Zondervan Publishing House. Pages 102-103.
3. This material is taken from *My Utmost for His Highest* by Oswald Chambers. © 1935 by Dodd Mead & Co., renewed © 1963 by the Oswald Chambers Publications Assn., Ltd., and is used by permission of Discovery House Publishers, Box 3566, Grand Rapids, Mich. 49501. All rights reserved. Page 306.

4. Debra Collins, on the last day of the Revive My Heart, O Lord pilot © 2000. Used by permission of the author.

WEEK 6, DAY 4

1. Alan Redpath, *Faith for the Times* (Grand Rapids, Mich.: Fleming H. Revell, a division of Baker Book House Company, 1972), pp. 53-54. Used by permission.
2. Brian Edwards, *Revival: A People Saturated with God* (Darlington, England: Evangelical Press, 1990), p. 48. Used by permission.
3. Spiros Zodhiates, *The Complete Word Study Old Testament* (Chattanooga, Tenn.: AMG Publishers, 1994), p. 2312.
4. Taken from *The Ssving Life of Christ*, by W. Ian Thomas. Copyright © 1961 by Zondervan Publishing House. Used by permission of Zondervan Publishing House. Page 19.

WEEK 6, DAY 5

1. Ruth Paxson, *Life on the Highest Plane* (Chicago: Moody, 1928), p. 43.
2. Herbert F. Stevenson, ed., *Keswick's Authentic Voice* (London: Marshall, Morgan & Scott, 1959), p. 376.
3. Alan Redpath, *Faith for the Times* (Grand Rapids, Mich.: Fleming H. Revell, a division of Baker Book House Company, 1972), pp. 44-45. Used by permission.
4. This material is taken from *My Utmost for His Highest* by Oswald Chambers. Copyright © 1935 by Dodd Mead & Co., renewed © 1963 by the Oswald Chambers Publications Assn., Ltd., and is used by permission of Discovery House Publishers, Box 3566, Grand Rapids, Mich. 49501. All rights reserved. Page 305.
5. Ruth Paxson, *Life on the Highest Plane* (Chicago: Moody, 1928), p. 57.

WEEK 6, DAYS 6–7

1. Brian Edwards, *Revival: A People Saturated with God* (Darlington, England: Evangelical Press, 1990), p. 71. Used by permission.

WEEK 7, DAY 1

1. Reprinted from *Daily Prayers*. Copyright © 1995 by F. B. Meyer, Harold Shaw Publishers, an imprint of WaterBrook Press, Colorado Springs, Colo. All rights reserved. Page 115.
2. E. M. Bounds, *E. M. Bounds on Prayer*. Copyright © 1997. Used by permission of Whitaker House, 30 Hunt Valley Circle, New Kensington, Penn. 15068. Pages 179-181.
3. R. A. Torrey, *How to Pray* (Old Tappan, N.J.: Fleming H. Revell, a division of Baker Book House Company, 1900), p. 53. Used by permission.

WEEK 7, DAY 2

1. Norman Grubb, *Rees Howells: Intercessor* (Fort Washington, Penn.: Christian Literature Crusade, 1952), p. 26.
2. E. M. Bounds, *E. M. Bounds on Prayer*. Copyright © 1997. Used by permission of Whitaker House, 30 Hunt Valley Circle, New Kensington, Penn. 15068. Page 148.

WEEK 7, DAY 3

1. Permission to copy was granted by Banner Of Truth, Carlisle, Penn., and taken from the book *The Valley of Vision*, Arthur Bennett, ed. Page 130.
2. Taken from *Enjoying Intimacy with God* by J. Oswald Sanders, Moody Press, copyright © 1980. Used with permission. Page 18.

WEEK 7, DAY 4

1. Reprinted from *Psalms: The Prayer Book of the Bible* by Dietrich Bonhoeffer. Copyright © 1970 Augsburg Publishing House. Used by permission of Augsburg Fortress. Pages 11-12.
2. This material is taken from *Prayer: A Holy Occupation* by Oswald Chambers. © 1992 by the Oswald Chambers Publications Assoc. Ltd., and is used by permission of Discovery House Publishers, Box 3566, Grand Rapids, Mich. 49501. All rights reserved. Page 184.

WEEK 7, DAY 5

1. E. M. Bounds, *E. M. Bounds on Prayer*. Copyright © 1997. Used by permission of Whitaker House, 30 Hunt Valley Circle, New Kensington, Penn. 15068. Page 556.
2. Bruce Wilkinson, *The Prayer of Jabez* (Sisters, Ore.: Multnomah, 2000), pp. 24-25. Used by permission.

WEEK 7, DAYS 6–7

1. Brian H. Edwards, *Revival: A People Saturated with God* (Darlington, England: Evangelical Press, 1990), p. 79. Used by permission.

WEEK 8, DAY 1

1. Taken from *They Found the Secret* by Mrs. Victor Raymond Edman. Copyright © 1960 by Zondervan Publishing House. Used by permission of Zondervan Publishing House. Page 88.

WEEK 8, DAY 2

1. F. B. Meyer, *Gospel of John* (Fort Washington, Penn.: Christian Literature Crusade, 1992), p. 289. Used by permission.

WEEK 8, DAY 3

1. Permission to copy was granted by Banner Of Truth, Carlisle, Penn., and taken from the book *The Valley of Vision*, Arthur Bennett, ed. Page 65.
2. Richard Sibbes, *The Bruised Reed* (1630; reprint Carlisle, Penn.: The Banner Of Truth Trust, 1998), pp. 125-126.

WEEK 8, DAY 4

1. Alan Redpath, *Blessings Out of Buffetings* (Old Tappan, N.J.: Fleming H. Revell, a division of Baker Book House Company, 1965), p. 213.
2. F. B. Meyer, *Gospel of John* (Fort Washington, Penn.: Christian Literature Crusade, 1970), p. 287-288. Used by permission.
3. Redpath, p. 213.

Week 8, Day 5

1. Herbert F. Stevenson, ed., *Keswick's Authentic Voice* (London: Marshall, Morgan & Scott, 1959), pp. 505-506.

Week 8, Days 6–7

1. From *The Coming World Revival* by Robert E. Coleman, copyright © 1989, pp. 80-81. Used by permission of Crossway Books, a division of Good News Publishers, Wheaton, Illinois 60187.

Week 9, Day 1

1. Herbert F. Stevenson, ed., *Keswick's Authentic Voice* (London: Marshall, Morgan & Scott, 1959), p. 511.

Week 9, Day 2

1. Leon Morris, *The Gospel According to John: The New International Commentary on the New Testament* (Grand Rapids, Mich.: Eerdmans, 1971), pp. 674-675.
2. Mrs. Charles Cowman, *Streams in the Desert* (Los Angeles: The Oriental Missionary Society, 1925), p. 300.

Week 9, Day 3

1. As seen under Mission Statement at www.ccci.org, the home of Campus Crusade for Christ on the Internet.
2. *Sharing the Abundant Life on Campus* (Orlando, Fla.: Campus Crusade for Christ International, 1972), p. vi.
3. Brian H. Edwards, *Revival: A People Saturated with God* (Darlington, England: Evangelical Press, 1990), p. 56. Used by permission.

Week 9, Day 4

1. Reprinted from *Daily Prayers*. Copyright © 1995 by F. B. Meyer, Harold Shaw Publishers, an imprint of WaterBrook Press, Colorado Springs, Colo. All rights reserved. Page 75.
2. Alan Redpath, *Blessings Out of Buffetings* (Old Tappan, N.J.: Fleming H. Revell, a division of Baker Book House Company, 1965), pp. 46-47. Used by permission.
3. A. W. Tozer, *Men Who Met God* (Camp Hill, Penn.: Christian Publications, 1986), pp. 121-122. Used by permission. For more information on these and other books by A. W. Tozer, call 1-800-233-4443 or visit Christian Publications' website at www.christianpublications.com.
4. A. W. Tozer, *The Pursuit of God* (Camp Hill, Penn.: Christian Publications, 1993), p. 128. Used by permission. For more information on these and other books by A. W. Tozer, call 1-800-233-4443 or visit Christian Publications' website at www.christianpublications.com.

Week 9, Day 5

1. Ruth Myers, *31 Days of Praise* (Sisters, Ore.: Multnomah, 1994), pp. 155-157. Used by permission.

2. A. W. Tozer, *Leaning into the Wind* (Wheaton, Ill.: Creation House, 1984), pp. 36-37. Used by permission.

3. Taken from *Enjoying Intimacy with God* by J. Oswald Sanders, Moody Press, copyright © 1980. Used with permission. Pages 24-26.

4. *Spiritual Disciplines for the Christian Life* by Donald Whitney, © 1991. Used by permission of NavPress Publishing. All rights reserved. For copies of the book call 800-366-7788. Pages 82-83.

5. Dick Eastman, *A Celebration of Praise* (Grand Rapids, Mich.: Baker Book House Company, 1984), p. 12. Used by permission.

WEEK 9, DAYS 6–7

1. *The Coming Revival* © Copyrighted 1995 by Bill Bright, *NewLife* Publications, Campus Crusade for Christ. All rights reserved. Used by permission.

2. A. W. Tozer, *The Pursuit of God* (Camp Hill, Penn.: Christian Publications, 1993), p. 17. Used by permission. For more information on these and other books by A. W. Tozer, call 1-800-233-4443 or visit Christian Publications' website at www.christianpublications.com.

3. Mrs. Charles Cowman, *Streams in the Desert* (Los Angeles: The Oriental Missionary Society, 1925), p. 301.

about the author

CATHERINE MARTIN is a summa cum laude graduate of Bethel Theological Seminary with a Master of Arts in Theological Studies. She is founder and president of Quiet Time Ministries, is director of Women's Ministries at Southwest Community Church in Indian Wells, California, is on the adjunct faculty of Biola University, and is dedicated to teaching devotion to God and His Word. Teaching at retreats and conferences, she challenges others to seek God and love Him with all of their hearts, souls, minds, and strength.